basic texts

of the
FOOD AND AGRICULTURE ORGANIZATION
OF THE UNITED NATIONS

Volumes I and II - 2000 edition

This 2000 edition includes all amendments adopted by the Conference up to November 1999. The Arabic, Chinese, English, French and Spanish texts are equally authoritative.

FAO Documentation Group Cataloguing in Publication Data

FAO, Rome (Italy)

Basic texts of the Food and Agriculture Organization
of the United Nations
(Volumes I and II – 2000 edition)
ISBN 92-5-104518-6

1. FAO 2. Administration
I. Title

FAO code: 90 Agris: D10

Printed in Italy

VOLUME I

Preamble

The Nations accepting this Constitution, being determined to promote the common welfare by furthering separate and collective action on their part for the purpose of:

raising levels of nutrition and standards of living of the peoples under their respective jurisdictions;

securing improvements in the efficiency of the production and distribution of all food and agricultural products;

bettering the condition of rural populations;

and thus contributing towards an expanding world economy and ensuring humanity's freedom from hunger;

hereby establish the Food and Agriculture Organization of the United Nations, hereinafter referred to as the "Organization" through which the Members will report to one another on the measures taken and the progress achieved in the field of action set forth above.

Article I

Functions of the Organization

1. The Organization shall collect, analyse, interpret and disseminate information relating to nutrition, food and agriculture. In this Constitution, the term "agriculture" and its derivatives include fisheries, marine products, forestry and primary forestry products.

2. The Organization shall promote and, where appropriate, shall recommend national and international action with respect to:

(*a*) scientific, technological, social and economic research relating to nutrition, food and agriculture;

(*b*) the improvement of education and administration relating to nutrition, food and agriculture, and the spread of public knowledge of nutritional and agricultural science and practice;

(*c*) the conservation of natural resources and the adoption of improved methods of agricultural production;

(*d*) the improvement of the processing, marketing and distribution of food and agricultural products;

(*e*) the adoption of policies for the provision of adequate agricultural credit, national and international;

(*f*) the adoption of international policies with respect to agricultural commodity arrangements.

3. It shall also be the function of the Organization:

(*a*) to furnish such technical assistance as governments may request;

(*b*) to organize, in cooperation with the governments concerned, such missions as may be needed to assist them to fulfil the obligation arising from their acceptance of the recommendations of the United Nations Conference on Food and Agriculture and of this Constitution; and

(*c*) generally to take all necessary and appropriate action to implement the purposes of the Organization as set forth in the Preamble.

Article II

Membership and Associate Membership

1. The original Member Nations of the Organization shall be such of the nations specified in Annex I as accept this Constitution, in accordance with the provisions of Article XXI.

2. The Conference may by a two-thirds majority of the votes cast, provided that a majority of the Member Nations of the Organization is present, decide to admit as an additional Member of the Organization any nation which has submitted an application for membership and a declaration made in a formal instrument that it will accept the obligations of the Constitution as in force at the time of admission.

3. The Conference may by a two-thirds majority of the votes cast, provided that a majority of the Member Nations of the Organization is present, decide to admit as a Member of the Organization any regional economic integration organization meeting the criteria set out in paragraph 4 of this Article, which has submitted an application for membership and a declaration made in a formal instrument that it will accept the obligations of the Constitution as in force at the time of admission. Subject to paragraph 8 of this Article, references to Member Nations under this Constitution shall include Member Organizations, except as otherwise expressly provided.

4. To be eligible to apply for membership of the Organization under paragraph 3 of this Article, a regional economic integration organization must be one constituted by sovereign States, a majority of which are Member Nations of the Organization, and to which its Member States have transferred competence over a range of matters within the purview of the Organization, including the authority to make decisions binding on its Member States in respect of those matters.

5. Each regional economic integration organization applying for membership in the Organization shall, at the time of such application, submit a declaration of competence specifying the matters in respect of which competence has been transferred to it by its Member States.

6. Member States of a Member Organization shall be presumed to retain competence over all matters in respect of which transfers of competence have not been specifically declared or notified to the Organization.

7. Any change regarding the distribution of competence between the Member Organization and its Member States shall be notified by the Member Organization or its Member States to the Director-General, who shall circulate such information to the other Member Nations of the Organization.

8. A Member Organization shall exercise membership rights on an alternative basis with its Member States that are Member Nations of the Organization in the areas of their respective competences and in accordance with rules set down by the Conference.

9. Except as otherwise provided in this Article, a Member Organization shall have the right to participate in matters within its competence in any meeting of the Organization, including any meeting of the Council or other body, other than bodies of restricted membership referred to below, in which any of

its Member States are entitled to participate. A Member Organization shall not be eligible for election or designation to any such body, nor shall it be eligible for election or designation to any body established jointly with other organizations. A Member Organization shall not have the right to participate in bodies of restricted membership specified in the rules adopted by the Conference.

10. Except as otherwise provided in this Constitution or in rules set down by the Conference, and Article III paragraph 4 notwithstanding, a Member Organization may exercise on matters within its competence, in any meeting of the Organization in which it is entitled to participate, a number of votes equal to the number of its Member States which are entitled to vote in such meeting. Whenever a Member Organization exercises its right to vote, its Member States shall not exercise theirs, and conversely.

11. The Conference may, under the same conditions regarding the required majority and quorum as prescribed in paragraph 2 above, decide to admit as an Associate Member of the Organization any territory or group of territories which is not responsible for the conduct of its international relations upon application made on its behalf by the Member Nation or authority having responsibility for its international relations, provided that such Member Nation or authority has submitted a declaration made in a formal instrument that it will accept on behalf of the proposed Associate Member the obligations of the Constitution as in force at the time of admission, and that it will assume responsibility for ensuring the observance of the provisions of paragraph 4 of Article VIII, paragraphs 1 and 2 of Article XVI, and paragraphs 2 and 3 of Article XVIII of this Constitution with regard to the Associate Member.

12. The nature and extent of the rights and obligations of Associate Members are defined in the relevant provision of this Constitution and the rules and regulations of the Organization.

13. Membership and Associate Membership shall become effective on the date on which the Conference approved the application.

Article III

The Conference

1. There shall be a Conference of the Organization in which each Member Nation and Associate Member shall be represented by one delegate. Associate

Members shall have the right to participate in the deliberations of the Conference but shall not hold office or have the right to vote.

2. Each Member Nation and Associate Member may appoint alternates, associates and advisers to its delegate. The Conference may determine the conditions for the participation of alternates, associates and advisers in its proceedings, but any such participation shall be without the right to vote, except in the case of an alternate, associate, or adviser participating in the place of a delegate.

3. No delegate may represent more than one Member Nation or Associate Member.

4. Each Member Nation shall have only one vote. A Member Nation which is in arrears in the payment of its financial contributions to the Organization shall have no vote in the Conference if the amount of its arrears equals or exceeds the amount of the contributions due from it for the two preceding calendar years. The Conference may, nevertheless, permit such a Member Nation to vote if it is satisfied that the failure to pay is due to conditions beyond the control of the Member Nation.

5. The Conference may invite any international organization which has responsibilities related to those of the Organization to be represented at its meetings on the conditions prescribed by the Conference. No representative of such an organization shall have the right to vote.

6. The Conference shall meet once in every two years in regular session. It may meet in special session:

(*a*) if at any regular session the Conference decides, by a majority of the votes cast, to meet in the following year;

(*b*) if the Council so instructs the Director-General, or if at least one-third of the Member Nations so request.

7. The Conference shall elect its own officers.

8. Except as otherwise expressly provided in this Constitution or by rules made by the Conference, all decisions of the Conference shall be taken by a majority of the votes cast.

Article IV

Functions of the Conference

1. The Conference shall determine the policy and approve the budget of the Organization and shall exercise the other powers conferred upon it by this Constitution.

2. The Conference shall adopt General Rules and Financial Regulations for the Organization.

3. The Conference may, by a two-thirds majority of the votes cast, make recommendations to Member Nations and Associate Members concerning questions relating to food and agriculture, for consideration by them with a view to implementation by national action.

4. The Conference may make recommendations to any international organization regarding any matter pertaining to the purpose of the Organization.

5. The Conference may review any decision taken by the Council or by any commission or committee of the Conference or Council, or by any subsidiary body of such commissions or committees.

Article V

Council of the Organization

1. A Council of the Organization consisting of forty-nine Member Nations shall be elected by the Conference. Each Member Nation on the Council shall have one representative and shall have only one vote. Each Member of the Council may appoint alternates, associates and advisers to its representative. The Council may determine the conditions for the participation of alternates, associates and advisers in its proceedings, but any such participation shall be without the right to vote, except in the case of an alternate, associate or adviser participating in the place of a representative. No representative may represent more than one Member of the Council. The tenure and other conditions of office of the Members of the Council shall be subject to rules made by the Conference.

2. The Conference shall, in addition, appoint an independent Chairman of the Council.

3. The Council shall have such powers as the Conference may delegate to it, but the Conference shall not delegate the powers set forth in paragraphs 2, 3 and 11 of Article II, Article IV, paragraph 1 of Article VII, Article XII, paragraph 4 of Article XIII, paragraphs 1 and 6 of Article XIV and Article XX of this Constitution.

4. The Council shall appoint its officers other than the Chairman and, subject to any decisions of the Conference, shall adopt its own Rules of Procedure.

5. Except as otherwise expressly provided in this Constitution or by rules made by the Conference or Council, all decisions of the Council shall be taken by a majority of the votes cast.

6. In the performance of its functions, the Council shall be assisted by a Programme Committee, a Finance Committee, a Committee on Constitutional and Legal Matters, a Committee on Commodity Problems, a Committee on Fisheries, a Committee on Forestry, a Committee on Agriculture and a Committee on World Food Security. These Committees shall report to the Council and their composition and terms of reference shall be governed by rules adopted by the Conference.

Article VI

Commissions, committees, conferences, working parties and consultations

1. The Conference or Council may establish commissions, the membership of which shall be open to all Member Nations and Associate Members, or regional commissions open to all Member Nations and Associate Members whose territories are situated wholly or in part in one or more regions, to advise on the formulation and implementation of policy and to coordinate the implementation of policy. The Conference or Council may also establish, in conjunction with other intergovernmental organizations, joint commissions open to all Member Nations and Associate Members of the Organization and of the other organizations concerned, or joint regional commissions open to Member Nations and Associate Members of the Organization and of the other

organizations concerned, whose territories are situated wholly or in part in the region.

2. The Conference, the Council, or the Director-General on the authority of the Conference or Council may establish committees and working parties to study and report on matters pertaining to the purpose of the Organization and consisting either of selected Member Nations and Associate Members, or of individuals appointed in their personal capacity because of their special competence in technical matters. The Conference, the Council, or the Director-General on the authority of the Conference or Council may, in conjunction with other intergovernmental organizations, also establish joint committees and working parties, consisting either of selected Member Nations and Associate Members of the Organization and of the other organizations concerned, or of individuals appointed in their personal capacity. The selected Member Nations and Associate Members shall, as regards the Organization, be designated either by the Conference or the Council, or by the Director-General if so decided by the Conference or Council. The individuals appointed in their personal capacity shall, as regards the Organization, be designated either by the Conference, the Council, selected Member Nations or Associate Members, or by the Director-General, as decided by the Conference or Council.

3. The Conference, the Council, or the Director-General on the authority of the Conference or Council shall determine the terms of reference and reporting procedures, as appropriate, of commissions, committees and working parties established by the Conference, the Council, or the Director-General as the case may be. Such commissions and committees may adopt their own rules of procedure and amendments thereto, which shall come into force upon approval by the Director-General. The terms of reference and reporting procedures of joint commissions, committees and working parties established in conjunction with other intergovernmental organizations shall be determined in consultation with the other organizations concerned.

4. The Director-General may establish, in consultation with Member Nations, Associate Members and National FAO Committees, panels of experts, with a view to developing consultation with leading technicians in the various fields of activity of the Organization. The Director-General may convene meetings of some or all of these experts for consultation on specific subjects.

5. The Conference, the Council, or the Director-General on the authority of the Conference or Council may convene general, regional, technical or other conferences, or working parties or consultations of Member Nations and

Associate Members, laying down their terms of reference and reporting procedures, and may provide for participation in such conferences, working parties and consultations, in such manner as they may determine, of national and international bodies concerned with nutrition, food and agriculture.

6. When the Director-General is satisfied that urgent action is required, he may establish the committees and working parties and convene the conferences, working parties and consultations provided for in paragraphs 2 and 5 above. Such action shall be notified by the Director-General to Member Nations and Associate Members and reported to the following session of the Council.

7. Associate Members included in the membership of the commissions, committees or working parties, or attending the conferences, working parties or consultations referred to in paragraphs 1, 2 and 5 above, shall have the right to participate in the deliberations of such commissions, committees, conferences, working parties and consultations, but shall not hold office or have the right to vote.

Article VII

The Director-General

1. There shall be a Director-General of the Organization who shall be appointed by the Conference for a term of six years. He shall be eligible for reappointment.

2. The appointment of the Director-General under this Article shall be made by such procedures and on such terms as the Conference may determine.

3. Should the office of Director-General become vacant prior to the expiry of his term of office, the Conference shall, either at the next regular session or at a special session convened in accordance with Article III, paragraph 6 of this Constitution, appoint a Director-General in accordance with the provisions of paragraphs 1 and 2 of this Article. However, the duration of the term of office of the Director-General appointed at a special session shall expire at the end of the year of the third regular session of the Conference following the date of his appointment.

4. Subject to the general supervision of the Conference and the Council, the Director-General shall have full power and authority to direct the work of the Organization.

5. The Director-General or a representative designated by him shall participate, without the right to vote, in all meetings of the Conference and of the Council and shall formulate for consideration by the Conference and the Council proposals for appropriate action in regard to matters coming before them.

Article VIII

Staff

1. The staff of the Organization shall be appointed by the Director-General in accordance with such procedure as may be determined by rules made by the Conference.

2. The staff of the Organization shall be responsible to the Director-General. Their responsibilities shall be exclusively international in character and they shall not seek or receive instructions in regard to the discharge thereof from any authority external to the Organization. The Member Nations and Associate Members undertake fully to respect the international character of the responsibilities of the staff and not to seek to influence any of their nationals in the discharge of such responsibilities.

3. In appointing the staff, the Director-General shall, subject to the paramount importance of securing the highest standards of efficiency and of technical competence, pay due regard to the importance of selecting personnel recruited on as wide a geographical basis as is possible.

4. Each Member Nation and Associate Member undertakes, insofar as it may be possible under its constitutional procedure, to accord to the Director-General and senior staff diplomatic privileges and immunities and to accord to other members of the staff all facilities and immunities accorded to nondiplomatic personnel attached to diplomatic missions or, alternatively, to accord to such other members of the staff the immunities and facilities which may hereafter be accorded to equivalent members of the staffs of other public international organizations.

Article IX

Seat

The seat of the Organization shall be determined by the Conference.

Article X

Regional and liaison offices

1. There shall be such regional offices and subregional offices as the Director-General, with the approval of the Conference, may decide.

2. The Director-General may appoint officials for liaison with particular countries or areas, subject to agreement of the government concerned.

Article XI

Reports by Member Nations and Associate Members

1. All Member Nations and Associate Members shall communicate regularly to the Director-General, on publication, the texts of laws and regulations pertaining to matters within the competence of the Organization which the Director-General considers useful for the purposes of the Organization.

2. With respect to the same matters, all Member Nations and Associate Members shall also communicate regularly to the Director-General statistical, technical and other information published or otherwise issued by, or readily available to, the government. The Director-General shall indicate from time to time the nature of the information which would be most useful to the Organization and the form in which this information might be supplied.

3. Member Nations and Associate Members may be requested to furnish, at such times and in such form as the Conference, the Council or the Director-General may indicate, other information, reports or documentation pertaining to matters within the competence of the Organization, including reports on the action taken on the basis of resolutions or recommendations of the Conference.

Article XII

Relations with the United Nations

1. The Organization shall maintain relations with the United Nations as a specialized agency within the meaning of Article 57 of the Charter of the United Nations.[1]

2. Agreements defining the relations between the Organization and the United Nations shall be subject to the approval of the Conference.

Article XIII

Cooperation with organizations and persons

1. In order to provide for close cooperation between the Organization and other international organizations with related responsibilities, the Conference may enter into agreements with the competent authorities of such organizations, defining the distribution of responsibilities and methods of cooperation.

2. The Director-General may, subject to any decision of the Conference, enter into agreements with other intergovernmental organizations for the maintenance of common services, for common arrangements in regard to recruitment, training, conditions of service and other related matters, and for interchanges of staff.

3. The Conference may approve arrangements placing other international organizations dealing with questions relating to food and agriculture under the

---

[1] Article 57 reads as follows: "1. The various specialized agencies, established by intergovernmental agreement and having wide international responsibilities, as defined, in their basic instruments, in economic, social, cultural, educational, health and related fields, shall be brought into relationship with the United Nations in accordance with the provisions of Article 63.

"2. Such agencies thus brought into relationship with the United Nations are hereinafter referred to as specialized agencies."

Article 63 reads as follows: "1. The Economic and Social Council may enter into agreements with any of the agencies referred to in Article 57, defining the terms on which the agency concerned shall be brought into relationship with the United Nations. Such agreements shall be subject to approval by the General Assembly.

"2. It may coordinate the activities of the specialized agencies through consultation with and recommendations to such agencies and through recommendations to the General Assembly and to the members of the United Nations."

general authority of the Organization on such terms as may be agreed with the competent authorities of the organization concerned.

4. The Conference shall make rules laying down the procedure to be followed to secure proper consultation with governments in regard to relations between the Organization and national institutions or private persons.

Article XIV

Conventions and agreements

1. The Conference may, by a two-thirds majority of the votes cast and in conformity with rules adopted by the Conference, approve and submit to Member Nations conventions and agreements concerning questions relating to food and agriculture.

2. The Council, under rules to be adopted by the Conference, may, by a vote concurred in by at least two thirds of the membership of the Council, approve and submit to Member Nations:

(*a*) agreements concerning questions relating to food and agriculture which are of particular interest to Member Nations of geographical areas specified in such agreements and are designed to apply only to such areas;

(*b*) supplementary conventions or agreements designed to implement any convention or agreement which has come into force under paragraphs 1 or 2 (*a*).

3. Conventions, agreements, and supplementary conventions and agreements shall:

(*a*) be submitted to the Conference or Council through the Director-General on behalf of a technical meeting or conference comprising Member Nations, which has assisted in drafting the convention or agreement and has suggested that it be submitted to Member Nations concerned for acceptance;

(*b*) contain provisions concerning the Member Nations of the Organization, and such non-member States as are members of the United Nations, any of its specialized agencies or the International Atomic Energy Agency, and regional economic integration organizations, including Member Organizations, to which their Member States have transferred competence over matters within the purview of the conventions, agreements, supplementary conventions and agreements, including the power to enter into treaties in respect thereto, which may become parties thereto and the number of acceptances by Member Nations necessary to bring such convention, agreement, supplementary convention or agreement into force, and thus to ensure that it will constitute a real contribution to the achievement of its objectives. In the case of conventions, agreements, supplementary conventions and agreements establishing commissions or committees, participation by non-member States of the Organization that are members of the United Nations, any of its specialized agencies or the International Atomic Energy Agency or by regional economic integration organizations other than Member Organizations, shall in addition be subject to prior approval by at least two-thirds of the membership of such commissions or committees. Where any convention, agreement, supplementary convention or agreement provides that a Member Organization or a regional economic integration organization that is not a Member Organization may become a party thereto, the voting rights to be exercised by such organizations and the other terms of participation shall be defined therein. Any such convention, agreement, supplementary convention or agreement shall, where the Member States of the organization do not participate in that convention, agreement, supplementary convention or agreement, and where other parties exercise one vote only, provide that the organization shall exercise only one vote in any body established by such convention, agreement, supplementary convention or agreement, but shall enjoy equal rights of participation with Member Nations parties to such convention, agreement, supplementary convention or agreement;

(*c*) not entail any financial obligations for Member Nations not parties to it other than their contributions to the Organization provided for in Article XVIII, paragraph 2 of this Constitution.

4. Any convention, agreement, supplementary convention or agreement approved by the Conference or Council for submission to Member Nations shall come into force for each contracting party as the convention, agreement, supplementary convention or agreement may prescribe.

5. As regards an Associate Member, conventions, agreements, supplementary conventions and agreements shall be submitted to the authority having responsibility for the international relations of the Associate Member.

6. The Conference shall make rules laying down the procedure to be followed to secure proper consultation with governments and adequate technical

preparations prior to consideration by the Conference or the Council of proposed conventions, agreements, supplementary conventions and agreements.

7. Two copies in the authentic language or languages of any convention, agreement, supplementary convention or agreement approved by the Conference or the Council shall be certified by the Chairman of the Conference or of the Council respectively and by the Director-General. One of these copies shall be deposited in the archives of the Organization. The other copy shall be transmitted to the Secretary-General of the United Nations for registration once the convention, agreement, supplementary convention or agreement has come into force as a result of action taken under this Article. In addition, the Director-General shall certify copies of those conventions, agreements, supplementary conventions or agreements and transmit one copy to each Member Nation of the Organization and to such non-member States or regional economic integration organizations as may become parties to the conventions, agreements, supplementary conventions or agreements.

Article XV

Agreements between the Organization and Member Nations

1. The Conference may authorize the Director-General to enter into agreements with Member Nations for the establishment of international institutions dealing with questions relating to food and agriculture.

2. In pursuance of a policy decision taken by the Conference by a two-thirds majority of the votes cast, the Director-General may negotiate and enter into such agreements with Member Nations subject to the provisions of paragraph 3 below.

3. The signature of such agreements by the Director-General shall be subject to the prior approval of the Conference by a two-thirds majority of the votes cast. The Conference may, in a particular case or cases, delegate the authority of approval to the Council, requiring a vote concurred in by at least two thirds of the membership of the Council.

Article XVI

Legal status

1. The Organization shall have the capacity of a legal person to perform any legal act appropriate to its purpose which is not beyond the powers granted to it by this Constitution.

2. Each Member Nation and Associate Member undertakes, insofar as it may be possible under its constitutional procedure, to accord to the Organization all the immunities and facilities which it accords to diplomatic missions, including inviolability of premises and archives, immunity from suit and exemptions from taxation.

3. The Conference shall make provision for the determination by an administrative tribunal of disputes relating to the conditions and terms of appointment of members of the staff.

Article XVII

Interpretation of the Constitution and settlement of legal questions

1. Any question or dispute concerning the interpretation of this Constitution, if not settled by the Conference, shall be referred to the International Court of Justice in conformity with the Statute of the Court or to such other body as the Conference may determine.

2. Any request by the Organization to the International Court of Justice for an advisory opinion on legal questions arising within the scope of its activities shall be in accordance with any agreement between the Organization and the United Nations.

3. The reference of any question or dispute under this Article, or any request for an advisory opinion, shall be subject to procedures to be prescribed by the Conference.

Article XVIII

Budget and contributions

1. The Director-General shall submit to each regular session of the Conference the budget of the Organization for approval.

2. Each Member Nation and Associate Member undertakes to contribute annually to the Organization its share of the budget, as apportioned by the Conference. When determining the contributions to be paid by Member Nations and Associate Members, the Conference shall take into account the difference in status between Member Nations and Associate Members.

3. Each Member Nation and Associate Member shall, upon approval of its application, pay as its first contribution a proportion, to be determined by the Conference, of the budget for the current financial period.

4. The financial period of the Organization shall be the two calendar years following the normal date for the regular session of the Conference, unless the Conference should otherwise determine.

5. Decisions on the level of the budget shall be taken by a two-thirds majority of the votes cast.

6. A Member Organization shall not be required to contribute to the budget as specified in paragraph 2 of this Article, but shall pay to the Organization a sum to be determined by the Conference to cover administrative and other expenses arising out of its membership in the Organization. A Member Organization shall not vote on the budget.

Article XIX

Withdrawal

Any Member Nation may give notice of withdrawal from the Organization at any time after the expiration of four years from the date of its acceptance of this Constitution. The notice of withdrawal of an Associate Member shall be given by the Member Nation or authority having responsibility for its international relations. Such notice shall take effect one year after the date of its communication to the Director-General. The financial obligation to the

Organization of a Member Nation which has given notice of withdrawal, or of an Associate Member on whose behalf notice of withdrawal has been given, shall include the entire calendar year in which the notice takes effect.

Article XX

Amendment of Constitution

1. The Conference may amend this Constitution by a two-thirds majority of the votes cast, provided that such majority is more than one half of the Member Nations of the Organization.

2. An amendment not involving new obligations for Member Nations or Associate Members shall take effect forthwith, unless the resolution by which it is adopted provides otherwise. Amendments involving new obligations shall take effect for each Member Nation and Associate Member accepting the amendment on acceptance by two thirds of the Member Nations of the Organization and thereafter for each remaining Member Nation or Associate Member on acceptance by it. As regards an Associate Member, the acceptance of amendments involving new obligations shall be given on its behalf by the Member Nation or authority having responsibility for the international relations of the Associate Member.

3. Proposals for the amendment of the Constitution may be made either by the Council or by a Member Nation in a communication addressed to the Director-General. The Director-General shall immediately inform all Member Nations and Associate Members of all proposals for amendments.

4. No proposal for the amendment of the Constitution shall be included in the agenda of any session of the Conference unless notice thereof has been dispatched by the Director-General to Member Nations and Associate Members at least 120 days before the opening of the session.

Article XXI

Entry into force of Constitution

1. This Constitution shall be open to acceptance by the nations specified in Annex I.

2. The instruments of acceptance shall be transmitted by each government to the United Nations Interim Commission on Food and Agriculture, which shall notify their receipt to the governments of the nations specified in Annex I. Acceptance may be notified to the Interim Commission through a diplomatic representative, in which case the instrument of acceptance must be transmitted to the Commission as soon as possible thereafter.

3. Upon the receipt by the Interim Commission of 20 notifications of acceptance, the Interim Commission shall arrange for this Constitution to be signed in a single copy by the diplomatic representatives duly authorized thereto of the nations who shall have notified their acceptance, and upon being so signed on behalf of not less than 20 of the nations specified in Annex I, this Constitution shall come into force immediately.

4. Acceptances, the notification of which is received after the entry into force of this Constitution, shall become effective upon receipt by the Interim Commission or the Organization.

Article XXII

Authentic texts of Constitution

The Arabic, Chinese, English, French and Spanish texts of this Constitution shall be equally authoritative.

Annex I

Nations eligible for original membership

Australia
Belgium
Bolivia
Brazil
Canada
Chile
China
Colombia
Costa Rica
Cuba
Czechoslovakia
Denmark
Dominican Republic
Ecuador
Egypt
El Salvador
Ethiopia
France
Greece
Guatemala
Haiti
Honduras
Iceland
India
Iran
Iraq
Liberia
Luxembourg
Mexico
Netherlands
New Zealand
Nicaragua
Norway
Panama
Paraguay
Peru
Philippine Commonwealth
Poland
Union of South Africa
Union of Soviet Socialist Republics
United Kingdom
United States of America
Uruguay
Venezuela
Yugoslavia

GENERAL RULES OF THE ORGANIZATION/B

A. THE CONFERENCE

Rule I

Sessions of the Conference

1. The regular session of the Conference shall be held at the seat of the Organization in the months of October or November, unless it is convened elsewhere or at a different time in pursuance of a decision of the Conference at a previous session, or, in exceptional circumstances, of a decision by the Council. For the purposes of the Constitution, of these Rules and of the Financial Regulations, the term "regular session" means the biennial session contemplated by paragraph 6 of Article III of the Constitution, and the terms "biennium" and "financial period" mean the two-year period starting on 1 January following the date on which the regular session of the Conference normally convenes in accordance with this paragraph. Any other session, whether convened in pursuance of a decision of the Conference or under paragraph 2 of this Rule, shall be a special session.

2. If the Council should so direct, or if at least one-third of the Member Nations should so request, the Director-General shall convene the Conference to meet in special session within six months of such direction or request at such time and place as the Council may designate.

3. Notices convening a regular session of the Conference shall be dispatched by the Director-General not less than 90 days, and notices convening a special session not less than 30 days, before the date fixed for the opening of the session, to Member Nations and Associate Members, and to the international organizations which may be represented at the Conference in pursuance of paragraph 5 of Article III of the Constitution, and of Rule XVII. These international organizations are hereafter referred to in these Rules as "participating international organizations".

Rule II

Agenda

Regular sessions

1. A provisional agenda for each regular session of the Conference shall be drawn up by the Director-General and dispatched to Member Nations and Associate Members and to participating international organizations not less than 90 days before the date fixed for the opening of the session.

2. The provisional agenda for a regular session shall include:

(*a*) all items the inclusion of which may have been decided upon by the Conference at a previous session;

(*b*) items approved by the Council after consultation with the Director-General; and

(*c*) (*i*) review of the state of food and agriculture and of the programmes of Member Nations and Associate Members, in the light of reports from the Council and the Director-General emphasizing policy issues which would require Conference consideration or which could be the subject of a formal recommendation by the Conference under paragraph 3 of Article IV of the Constitution;

(*ii*) a report by the Director-General on the work of the Organization;

(*iii*) the Director-General's draft programme of work and budgetary proposals for the ensuing financial period, together with a report by the Council on the audited final accounts of the Organization for the preceding financial period;

(*iv*) review of the activities of the Organization undertaken under the United Nations Development Programme and formulation of views for the guidance of the Director-General regarding the lines along which these activities should develop;

(*v*) a report by the Council on its work;

(*vi*) applications for admission of additional Member Nations or Associate Members to the Organization, if any, in accordance with Rule XIX;

(*vii*) election of Members of the Council and appointment of the

Chairman of the Council in accordance with Rules XXII and XXIII;

(*viii*) amendments to the Constitution, if any, in accordance with Article XX of the Constitution;

(*ix*) any item the inclusion of which has been agreed to by the Council, after consultation with the Director-General, upon the request of the United Nations or a specialized agency of the United Nations;

(*x*) re-examination of the scale of contributions, if recommended or requested, under Rule XX, paragraph (*d*).

Special sessions

3. A provisional agenda for each special session of the Conference shall be drawn up by the Director-General and dispatched to Member Nations and Associate Members and to participating international organizations not less than 30 days before the date fixed for the opening of the session.

4. The provisional agenda for a special session shall include:

(*a*) all items the inclusion of which in the agenda of the special session may have been decided upon by the Conference at a previous session;

(*b*) items approved by the Council, after consultation with the Director-General;

(*c*) any items proposed for consideration in any request by one third of the Member Nations for the holding of the session, under Rule I, paragraph 2;

(*d*) the filling of any vacancies on the Council, under Rule XXII, paragraph 6;

(*e*) applications for admission of additional Member Nations or Associate Members to the Organization, if any, in accordance with Rule XIX.

Regular and special sessions

5. Any Member Nation or Associate Member acting within the limits of its status may, not less than 30 days before the date fixed for the opening of a session, request the Director-General to include specific items on the agenda. These items shall be placed on a supplementary list, which shall be dispatched

to Member Nations and Associate Members not less than 20 days before the date fixed for the opening of the session, and shall be presented to the General Committee for recommendation to the Conference.

6. During any session the Conference may, by a two-thirds majority of the votes cast, add to the agenda any item proposed by a Member Nation or an Associate Member acting within the limits of its status. No such item shall be considered in the absence of a report by the Director-General on its technical, administrative and financial implications, if any, unless the Conference shall otherwise decide in a case of urgency.

7. Proposals by Member Nations or Associate Members for the agenda of any session of the Conference, if not made at a session, shall be made to the Director-General, who shall present them to the General Committee together with a report on their technical, administrative and financial implications, if any. All agenda proposals made by Member Nations or Associate Members shall be accompanied by explanatory memoranda and, if possible, by basic documents or, where appropriate, by draft resolutions.

8. Where an item proposed for the agenda of a session of the Conference in conformity with these Rules contains a proposal for new activities to be undertaken by the Organization relating to matters which are of direct concern to the United Nations, one or more of the specialized agencies of the United Nations or other intergovernmental organizations with which the Organization has an Agreement of Relationship, the Director-General shall enter into consultation with the organizations concerned and report to the Conference on the means of achieving coordinated use of the resources of the respective organizations. Where a proposal put forward in the course of a session for new activities to be undertaken by the Organization relates to matters which are of direct concern to the United Nations or one or more of the other organizations referred to above, the Director-General shall, after such consultation as may be possible with the representative of the other organization concerned attending the session, draw the attention of the Conference to the interest which the other organization or organizations may have in the proposal. Before deciding on such proposals, the Conference shall either satisfy itself that adequate consultations have taken place with the organizations concerned or arrange for such consultations.

9. Copies of all reports and other documents to be submitted to the Conference at any session, in connection with any item which may be on the agenda, shall be furnished by the Director-General to the Member Nations and

Associate Members and to participating international organizations, at the same time as the agenda or as soon as possible thereafter, except as may be otherwise provided in these Rules and the Financial Regulations. The Director-General's draft programme of work and budgetary proposals for the ensuing financial period shall, where practicable, be accompanied by the joint report of the Programme and Finance Committees, provided for in Rule XXVIII, paragraph 3 of these Rules.

10. The Conference shall not proceed to the discussion of any item on the agenda until at least 72 hours have elapsed since the documents referred to in paragraph 6 or 9, as the case may be, have been made available to delegations.

11. At each session the provisional agenda, together with items on the supplementary list, if any, which have been approved by the General Committee, shall be submitted to the Conference for approval as soon as possible after the opening of the session and, on approval of the Conference with or without amendment, shall become the agenda of the Conference.

Rule III

Delegations and credentials

1. For the purpose of these Rules the term "delegation" means all the persons appointed by a Member Nation or an Associate Member to attend a session of the Conference, that is to say, its delegate and his alternates, associates and advisers.

2. The credentials of delegates, alternates, associates and advisers, and of the representatives of the participating international organizations shall, insofar as possible, be deposited with the Director-General not less than 15 days before the date fixed for the opening of each session of the Conference. The credentials of delegates, alternates, associates and advisers shall be issued by, or on behalf of, the head of state, the head of government, the minister of foreign affairs or the minister concerned. A Permanent Representative to the Organization does not require special credentials if his letter of accreditation to the Organization specifies that he is authorized to represent his government at sessions of the Conference, it being understood that this would not preclude that government from accrediting another delegate by means of special credentials.

3. There shall be a Credentials Committee of the Conference consisting of nine Member Nations.

4. The Credentials Committee shall examine the credentials deposited in accordance with paragraph 2 and report promptly thereon to the Conference, which shall decide any questions arising.

5. Any delegation or representative to whose admission a Member Nation has made objection shall be seated provisionally with the same rights as other delegations or representatives until the Credentials Committee has reported and the Conference has given its decision.

6. The Chairman of the Credentials Committee shall be elected by the Committee. He shall have, in relation to meetings of the Committee, the same powers and duties as the Chairman of the Conference in relation to meetings of the Conference. A majority of the members of the Committee shall constitute a quorum. Decisions in the Committee shall be taken by a majority of the votes cast. No member shall have more than one vote. Meetings of the Committee shall be held in private unless otherwise determined by the Conference.

Rule IV

Secretariat

1. The Director-General shall provide and direct such Secretariat and other staff and facilities as may be required by the Conference and by such commissions or committees as it may establish.

2. It shall be the duty of the Secretariat to receive, translate and circulate documents, reports and resolutions of the Conference and of its commissions and committees; to prepare the records of the proceedings; and to perform such other work as the Conference or any of its commissions or committees may require.

Rule V

Attendance at plenary meetings of the Conference

1. Plenary meetings of the Conference shall be open to attendance by all

delegations, the representatives of participating international organizations, and such members of the staff of the Organization as the Director-General may designate.

2. Plenary meetings of the Conference shall be held in public unless the Conference decides otherwise.

3. Subject to any decision of the Conference, the Director-General shall make arrangements for the admission of the public and of representatives of the press and other information agencies to plenary meetings of the Conference.

Rule VI

Opening of the session

At the opening of each session of the Conference, the Director-General shall preside until the Conference has elected a Chairman.

Rule VII

Nominations

The Chairman of the Conference, the chairmen of the commissions of the Conference, the three Vice-Chairmen of the Conference, the members of the Credentials Committee and the elected members of the General Committee, provided for by Rule X, paragraph 1 shall be nominated by the Council.

Rule VIII

Election of Chairman and Vice-Chairmen of the Conference and of the members of the Credentials and General Committees

The Conference shall, after consideration of the Report of the Council, elect:

(*a*) from the delegations, a Chairman and three Vice-Chairmen;

(*b*) from the Member Nations:

(*i*) the Credentials Committee, as provided in Rule III, paragraph 3;

(*ii*) the seven members of the General Committee to be elected as provided in Rule X, paragraph 1.

Rule IX

Powers and duties of Chairman and Vice-Chairmen of the Conference

1. In addition to exercising such powers as are conferred upon him elsewhere by these Rules, the Chairman shall declare the opening and closing of each plenary meeting of the session. He shall direct the discussions in plenary meetings, and at such meetings ensure observance of these Rules, accord the right to speak, put questions and announce decisions. He shall rule on points of order and, subject to these Rules, shall have complete control over the proceedings at any meetings. He may, in the course of the discussion of an item, propose to the Conference the limitation of the time to be allowed to speakers, the number of times each delegation may speak on any question, the closure of the list of speakers, the suspension or adjournment of the meeting, or the adjournment or closure of the debate on the item under discussion.

2. In the absence of the Chairman during a plenary meeting or any part thereof, one of the Vice-Chairmen shall preside. A Vice-Chairman acting as Chairman shall have the same powers and duties as the Chairman.

3. The Chairman, or a Vice-Chairman acting as Chairman, shall not vote but may appoint an alternate, associate or adviser from his delegation to vote in his place.

4. The Chairman, in the exercise of his functions, remains under the authority of the Conference.

Rule X

General Committee

1. There shall be a General Committee of the Conference consisting of the Chairman and Vice-Chairmen of the Conference and seven Member Nations

elected by the Conference under Rule VIII. The Chairman of the Conference shall be the Chairman of the Committee. He shall have, in relation to meetings of the Committee, the same powers and duties as he has in relation to meetings of the Conference. In the absence of the Chairman during a meeting of the General Committee, or any part thereof, one of the Vice-Chairmen shall preside. A Vice-Chairman acting as Chairman shall have the same powers and duties as the Chairman. A majority of the members of the Committee shall constitute a quorum. Decisions in the Committee shall be taken by a majority of the votes cast. No member shall have more than one vote. Meetings of the Committee shall be held in private unless otherwise determined by the Conference.

2. In addition to exercising such duties as are specified elsewhere in these Rules, the General Committee shall, in consultation with the Director-General and subject to any decision of the Conference:

(*a*) arrange the time and place of all plenary meetings and of all meetings of commissions and committees established at plenary meetings during the session;

(*b*) determine the order of business at each plenary meeting of the session;

(*c*) propose the allocation to the different commissions and committees of the Conference of the various items of the agenda and propose the vice-chairmen of the commissions;

(*d*) meet periodically throughout each session to review the progress of the Conference, to coordinate the work of all commissions and committees and to make recommendations for furthering such progress; and meet at such other times as the Chairman deems necessary or upon the request of any other of its members;

(*e*) report on any additions to the agenda proposed during the session under Rule II, paragraph 6;

(*f*) fix the date of adjournment of the session;

(*g*) report to the Conference on any request by a participating international non-governmental organization to speak before a plenary meeting of the session (Rule XVII, paragraph 3);

(*h*) report to the Conference on applications for admission to membership and associate membership in the Organization (Rule XIX);

(*i*) make recommendations to the Conference on the election of members of the Council, formally draw the attention of the Conference to the provisions of paragraphs 3 and 4 of Rule XXII, and generally carry out its responsibilities with respect to the election of members of the Council as provided for in that Rule;

(*j*) determine and announce the date of election of the Chairman of the Council, and of the Director-General, as soon as possible after the opening of the Conference session, and submit to the Conference recommendations with respect to the conditions of their appointment [Rules XXIII, paragraph 1 and XXXVI, paragraph 1 (*c*)];

(*k*) otherwise facilitate the orderly dispatch of the business of the session.

3. The reports of all commissions and committees established to consider items of the agenda of any session of the Conference and the report of the session shall, before being submitted at a plenary meeting for final decision thereon at that session, be referred to the General Committee for coordination and editing and for such procedural recommendation as the General Committee may wish to make. Such reports, including draft resolutions and any recommendations of the General Committee, shall thereafter be circulated, insofar as is practicable, at least 24 hours in advance of the plenary meeting at which they are to be considered.

4. A Member Nation which is not represented on the General Committee or an Associate Member, either of which has requested the inclusion of an item on the agenda of the Conference in accordance with the provisions of Rule II, may attend any meeting of the General Committee at which its request is discussed, and may participate, without vote, in the discussion of the item.

Rule XI

Proposals and amendments

1. Proposals relating to an item on the agenda shall be introduced in or referred to the commission or committee to which the relevant item has been allocated, except where the item concerned is to be considered at plenary meetings without prior referral to a commission or committee.

2. Proposals and amendments shall be introduced in writing and handed to the Secretary-General of the Conference, who shall arrange for their circulation as Conference documents.

3. Except as may be decided otherwise by the Conference at a plenary

meeting or by a commission or committee, proposals shall not be put to the vote unless copies thereof have been circulated at least twenty-four hours before the vote. The Chairman of the Conference or of the commission or committee concerned may permit voting on amendments even though these amendments have not been circulated or have been circulated less than twenty-four hours before the vote.

4. A proposal may be withdrawn at any time before voting on it has commenced, provided that the proposal has not been amended. A proposal which has thus been withdrawn may be reintroduced by any member.

Rule XII

Quorum and voting arrangements at meetings of Conference and Council

1. Subject to the Constitution and these Rules, the following shall govern the procedure in relation to voting and elections in the Conference and the Council:

2. (*a*) Except as otherwise provided by the Constitution or these Rules, in the Conference a majority of the Member Nations and in the Council a majority of the Members of the Council shall constitute a quorum.

(*b*) Before proceeding to a vote or election, the Chairman shall announce the number of delegates or representatives present. If less than the number required for a quorum is present, the vote or election shall not be held.

3. (*a*) Except as otherwise provided in the Constitution or these Rules, the required majority for any decision or for any election to fill one elective place shall be more than one half of the votes cast.

(*b*) Except as otherwise provided in these Rules, in the case of an election by the Conference to fill simultaneously more than one elective place, the required majority shall be the smallest number of whole votes necessary to elect no more candidates than there are seats to be filled. This majority shall be obtained by the following formula:

$$\text{Required majority} = \frac{\text{number of votes cast}}{\text{number of seats} + 1} + 1$$

(disregarding any resultant fraction).

(*c*) Subject to the provisions of Article XX, paragraph 1 of the Constitution, when a two-thirds majority of the votes cast is required by the Constitution or these Rules for a decision to be taken by the Conference, the total number of affirmative and negative votes cast shall be more than one half of the Member Nations of the Organization. If these conditions are not fulfilled, the proposal shall be considered as rejected.[1]

4. (*a*) For the purpose of the Constitution and these Rules the phrase "votes cast" shall mean affirmative and negative votes, and shall not include abstentions or defective ballots.

(*b*) In the case of an election to fill simultaneously more than one elective place the phrase "votes cast" shall mean the total number of votes cast by the electors for all elective places.

(*c*) Abstentions shall be recorded:

(*i*) in a vote by show of hands, only for those delegates or representatives who raise their hands in response to the Chairman's request for abstentions;

(*ii*) in a roll call vote, only for those delegates or representatives who reply "Abstention";

(*iii*) in a secret ballot, only for such ballot papers deposited in the ballot box as are either blank or marked "Abstention";

(*iv*) in a vote by electronic means, only for those delegates or representatives who indicate "Abstention".

---

[1] The following are the cases in which, for a decision to be taken by the Conference, a two-thirds majority of the votes cast is required, provided that the total number of affirmative and negative votes cast shall be more than one half of the Member Nations of the Organization:

- Admission of additional or Associate Members.
- Approval of conventions and agreements.
- Approval of agreements between the Organization and Member Governments.
- Decisions on the level of the budget.
- Formulation of recommendations to Member Governments.
- Inclusion of new items on the Conference agenda after it has been formally adopted by the Conference.
- Amendment or suspension of the General Rules of the Organization.

In the case of amendments by the Conference to the Constitution, a two-thirds majority of the votes cast is also required, provided that such majority is more than one half of the Member Nations of the Organization.

In the case of approval of agreements and supplementary conventions and agreements by the Council and the addition of items to the Council's agenda during a session, a two-thirds majority of the membership of the Council is required (i.e., at least 33 Council Members in favour).

(*d*) (*i*) Any ballot paper carrying votes for more candidates than there are vacancies to be filled, or carrying a vote for an individual, nation or locality not validly nominated, shall be considered defective.

(*ii*) In the case of an election to fill simultaneously more than one elective place any ballot paper carrying votes for less candidates than there are vacancies to be filled shall also be considered defective.

(*iii*) The ballot paper shall carry no other notation or mark than those required for the purpose of indicating the vote.

(*iv*) Subject to (*i*), (*ii*) and (*iii*) above, a ballot paper shall be considered valid when there is no doubt as to the intention of the elector.

5. Except as otherwise provided in the Constitution or these Rules, the nomination of any candidate for an elective place to be filled by the Conference or Council shall be made by the government of a Member Nation or by its delegate or representative. Subject to the procedure for nomination provided in the Rules, the appointing body shall determine the nomination procedure.

6. Voting shall be by show of hands, roll call or secret ballot.

7. (*a*) Subject to the provisions of paragraph 10 of this Rule, a vote by roll call shall be taken either upon request of a delegate or representative, or if a majority of two thirds is required by the Constitution or these Rules. Voting by roll call shall be conducted by calling in English alphabetical order the names of all Member Nations entitled to vote. The name of the first nation to be called shall be designated by lot drawn by the Chairman. The delegate or representative of each Member Nation shall reply "Yes", "No", or "Abstention". At the conclusion of any roll call, the name of any Member Nation whose delegate or representative failed to answer shall be called again. The vote of each Member Nation participating in any vote by roll call shall be inserted in the record of the meeting.

(*b*) The count and recording of votes by show of hands or by roll call shall be conducted by or under the supervision of the Conference or Council elections officer, appointed by the Director-General in accordance with the terms of paragraph 17 below.

(*c*) If for two successive ballots by roll call the name of the same Member Nation is drawn, the name of another Member Nation shall be designated by lot or lots drawn by the Chairman.

8. When the Conference or Council votes by electronic means, a vote without recording names shall replace a vote by show of hands and a nominal vote shall replace a roll call. In the case of a nominal vote, the procedure of calling out the names of the Member Nations shall not be applicable unless the Conference or Council otherwise decides. The vote of each Member Nation participating in a nominal vote shall be inserted in the record.

9. (*a*) For the purpose of the Rules, the term "election" means the selection or appointment of one or more individuals, nations or localities. The election of Council Members shall take place in accordance with the procedure laid down in Rule XXII, paragraph 10 (*g*). In other cases, more than one elective place shall be filled at the same election, unless the Conference or Council decide otherwise.

(*b*) When one elective place is to be filled, the method of election by secret ballot shall be as provided in paragraph 11 of this Rule. When more than one elective place is to be filled at the same election, the method of election by secret ballot shall be as provided in paragraphs 12 and 13 of this Rule.

10. (*a*) The appointment of the Chairman of the Council and of the Director-General, the admission of additional Member Nations and Associate Members shall be decided by secret ballot. Other elections shall likewise be decided by secret ballot, except that in the case of an election in which there are not more candidates than vacancies the Chairman may submit to the Conference or Council that the appointment be decided by clear general consent.

(*b*) Any other matter shall be decided by secret ballot if the Conference or Council so determines.

(*c*) (*i*) For the purpose of a secret ballot the Chairman of the Conference or Council shall appoint two tellers from among the delegates or representatives, or their alternates. In the case of a secret ballot for an election, the tellers shall be delegates or representatives, or their alternates, who are not parties directly interested in the election.

(*ii*) The duties of the tellers shall be to supervise the balloting procedure, count the ballot papers, decide on the validity of a ballot paper in any case of doubt, and certify the result of each ballot.

(*iii*) The same tellers may be appointed for successive ballots or elections.

(*d*) Ballot papers shall be duly initialled by an authorized officer of the secretariat of the Conference or Council. The elections officer shall be responsible for ensuring compliance with this requirement. For each ballot only one blank ballot paper shall be given to each delegation entitled to vote.

(*e*) For a vote by secret ballot, one or more voting booths shall be set up, supervised in such a manner as to ensure complete secrecy of the ballot.

(*f*) Should any delegate invalidate his ballot paper, he may, before leaving the precinct of the polling booths, request a new blank ballot paper, which shall be delivered to him by the elections officer on the surrender of the invalidated ballot paper. The invalidated ballot paper shall remain in the custody of the elections officer.

(*g*) Should the tellers withdraw from the presence of the delegates or representatives in order to carry out the count of the votes, only the candidates or scrutineers appointed by the candidates may attend the count, but they shall not take part in the count.

(*h*) Members of delegations and of the secretariat of the Conference or Council who are responsible for the supervision of any vote by secret ballot shall not disclose to any unauthorized person any information which might tend, or be presumed to tend, towards destroying the secrecy of the ballot.

(*i*) The Director-General shall be responsible for the safe custody of all ballot papers until the elected candidates take office or for three months after the date of the ballot, whichever is the longer period.

11. In any election for one elective place, other than that of the Director-General, if a candidate fails on the first ballot to obtain a majority of the votes cast, successive ballots shall be taken at such time or times as the Conference or Council shall decide, until a candidate obtains such a majority.

12. In any election by the Conference to fill simultaneously more than one elective place the following shall apply:

(*a*) Each elector, unless he wholly abstains, shall cast one vote for each elective place to be filled. Each vote shall be cast for a different candidate. Any ballot paper which is not in conformity with these requirements shall be declared defective.

(*b*) Any candidate who receives the required majority of the votes cast as defined in paragraph 3 (*b*) of this Rule shall be declared elected.

(*c*) If only some of the elective places have been filled after the first ballot, a second ballot shall be cast to fill the remaining elective places, under the same conditions as the first ballot.

(*d*) This procedure shall continue until all the elective places have been filled.

(*e*) If in any ballot no candidate received the required majority, the candidate having received the smallest number of votes in that ballot shall be eliminated and a further ballot held, in accordance with (*c*) above, between the remaining candidates.

(*f*) If in any ballot no candidate receives the required majority and more than one candidate receives the smallest number of votes, a separate ballot between these candidates shall be held and the candidate receiving the smallest number of votes shall be eliminated.

(*g*) If in the separate ballot provided for in (*f*) of this paragraph more than one candidate again receives the smallest number of votes, the above operation shall be repeated with respect to those candidates until one candidate is eliminated, provided that if all the same candidates receive the smallest number of votes in two successive separate ballots, such candidates as will have been designated by lot shall be eliminated.

(*h*) If at any stage in an election other than a separate ballot all remaining candidates receive the same number of votes, the Chairman of the Conference shall formally announce that if in the two following ballots the votes are again equally divided he will suspend balloting for a period which he shall determine and then hold two further ballots. If after applying this procedure the final ballot again results in an equally divided vote, such candidate as will have been designated by lot shall be declared elected.

13. In any election by the Council to fill simultaneously more than one elective place, the following shall apply:

(*a*) Two thirds of the membership of the Council shall constitute a quorum and more than one half of the number of Council Members casting valid votes shall constitute the required majority.

(*b*) Each elector, unless he wholly abstains, shall cast one vote for each elective place to be filled. Each vote shall be cast for a different candidate. Any ballot paper which is not in conformity with these requirements shall be declared defective.

(*c*) The candidates who receive the largest number of votes shall be declared elected in a number equal to the number of elective places to be filled, provided they have received the required majority defined in paragraph (*a*) above.

(*d*) If only some of the elective places have been filled after the first ballot, a second ballot shall be cast to fill the remaining elective places, under the same conditions as the first ballot. This procedure shall be continued until all the elective places have been filled.

(*e*) If, at any stage during the election, one or more of the vacant elective places cannot be filled because of an equal number of votes having been obtained by two or more candidates, a separate ballot shall be held among such candidates to determine which of them will be elected, in accordance with the provisions of paragraph (*c*) above. Such procedure will be repeated if necessary.

14. (*a*) If a vote is equally divided on a matter other than an election, a second vote shall be taken at a subsequent meeting to be held not less than one hour after the conclusion of the meeting at which the equally divided vote occurred. If the second vote is also equally divided the proposal shall be regarded as rejected.

(*b*) At any stage in an election after the first ballot has been held, further balloting may be postponed by the Chairman with the concurrence of the Conference or Council.

15. Once voting has commenced, no delegate or representative may interrupt the voting except to rise to a point of order in connection with the voting.

16. (*a*) Any delegate or representative may challenge the result of a vote or election.

(*b*) In the case of a vote by show of hands or roll call vote, should the result be challenged, the Chairman shall cause a second vote to be taken forthwith.

(*c*) A vote by show of hands or by roll call may be challenged only immediately after the result has been announced.

(*d*) A secret ballot may be challenged at any time within three months of the date upon which it took place or until the elected candidate takes office, whichever is the longer period.

(*e*) Should a vote or election by secret ballot be challenged, the Director-General shall cause the ballot papers and all relevant record sheets to be re-examined and shall circulate the result of the investigation, together with the original complaint, to all Member Nations of the Organization or of the Council, as appropriate.

17. An officer of the Secretariat designated by the Director-General for each Conference or Council session, who shall be known as the elections officer, shall, with the assistance of a deputy or deputies, be responsible for the following duties:

(*a*) to ensure that the provisions of the Constitution and the General Rules of the Organization regarding voting and electoral procedure are correctly carried out;

(*b*) to be responsible for all arrangements for voting and elections;

(*c*) to advise the Chairman of the Conference or Council on all matters pertaining to voting procedures and mechanics;

(*d*) to supervise the preparation of ballot papers and be responsible for their safe custody;

(*e*) to report to the Chairman of the Conference or Council the presence of a quorum before any vote is taken;

(*f*) to maintain records of all election results, ensuring that they are faithfully recorded and published;

(*g*) to undertake such other relevant duties as may arise in connection with voting and elections.

18. If a decision is to be taken on a matter other than an election, for which a two-thirds majority is not required by the Constitution or these Rules, the Chairman may submit to the Conference or Council that the matter be decided by general consent without recourse to a formal vote.

19. Parts of a proposal or of an amendment shall be voted on separately if a delegate or representative requests such division, provided that, if objection is made, the question of division shall be decided by the Conference or Council. In addition to the delegate or representative requesting the division, two delegates or two representatives may speak for, and two against, the motion for division. If the motion for division is carried, those parts of the proposal or

of the amendment which are subsequently approved shall be put to the vote as a whole. If all operative parts of the proposal or of the amendment have been rejected, the proposal or the amendment shall be considered to have been rejected as a whole.

20. The Conference or Council may limit the time to be allowed to each speaker and the number of times any delegate or representative may speak on any question. When debate is limited and a delegate or representative has spoken his allotted time, the Chairman shall call him to order without delay.

21. During the discussion of any matter, a delegate or representative may rise to a point of order and the point of order shall be immediately decided by the Chairman. A delegate or representative may appeal against the ruling of the Chairman, in which event the appeal shall immediately be put to the vote and the Chairman's ruling shall stand unless overruled by a majority of the votes cast. A delegate or representative rising to a point of order may not speak on the substance of the matter under discussion.

22. During the discussion of any matter, a delegate or representative may move the suspension or adjournment of the meeting. Such motion shall not be debated but shall be immediately put to the vote. The Chairman may limit the time to be allowed to the speaker moving the suspension or adjournment of the meeting. At any meeting the same delegate or representative may not move the suspension or adjournment of the meeting more than once during the discussion of any one matter.

23. During the discussion of any matter, a delegate or representative may move the adjournment of the debate on the item under discussion. In addition to the proposer of the motion, two delegates or two representatives may speak for, and two against, the motion, after which the motion shall be immediately put to the vote. The Chairman may limit the time allowed to these speakers.

24. A delegate or representative may at any time move the closure of the debate on the item under discussion, whether or not any other delegate or representative has signified his wish to speak. Permission to speak on the closure of the debate shall be accorded only to two speakers opposing the closure, after which the motion shall be immediately put to the vote. If the Conference or Council is in favour of the closure, the Chairman shall declare the closure of the debate. The Chairman may limit the time allowed to speakers under this paragraph.

25. The following motions shall have precedence in the following order over all other proposals or motions before the meeting, except a point of order:

(*a*) to suspend the meeting;

(*b*) to adjourn the meeting;

(*c*) to adjourn the debate on the item under discussion; and

(*d*) for the closure of the debate on the item under discussion.

26. When a proposal has been adopted or rejected, it may not be reconsidered at the same session unless the Conference or Council so decides. Permission to speak on a motion to reconsider shall be accorded only to two speakers opposing the motion, after which it shall be immediately put to the vote.

27. When an amendment to a proposal is moved, the amendment shall be voted on first. When two or more amendments to a proposal are moved, the Conference or Council shall first vote on the amendment deemed by the Chairman to be furthest removed in substance from the original proposal, and then on the amendment next removed therefrom, and so on, until all the amendments have been put to the vote. Where, however, the adoption of one amendment necessarily implies the rejection of another, the latter shall not be put to the vote. If one or more amendments are adopted, the amended proposal shall then be voted upon. A motion is considered an amendment to a proposal if it merely adds to, deletes from, or revises part of that proposal, but not if it negatives the proposal. An amendment by way of substitute shall not be voted on until the vote has been taken on the original proposal and any amendments thereto.

28. Subject to paragraph 27, any motion calling for a decision by the Conference or Council on its competence to adopt a proposal submitted to it shall be put to the vote before a vote is taken on the proposal in question.

29. Associate Members shall have the right to participate with Member Nations in matters pertaining to the conduct of business of meetings of the Conference, its commissions and committees, in accordance with the provisions of the foregoing paragraphs of this Rule, subject, however, to the limitations on voting and the holding of office stipulated in paragraph 1 of Article III of the Constitution, paragraph 3 of Rule XIII, paragraph 1 of Rule XIV and paragraph 1 of Rule XV of the General Rules of the Organization.

Rule XIII

Commissions of the Conference

1. The Conference may set up at each session such commissions as it considers desirable and, after consideration of the recommendations of the General Committee, shall allocate to these commissions the various items on its agenda.

2. The Conference shall, after consideration of the recommendations of the Council and the General Committee, elect a chairman and one or more vice-chairmen for each commission.

3. Each delegate shall be entitled to sit or be represented by another member of his delegation on each such commission and may be accompanied at meetings by one or more members of his delegation, who may speak but shall not vote. Delegates of Associate Members shall have the right to participate in the deliberations of each such commission, but shall not hold office or have the right to vote.

4. The chairman of each commission shall have in relation to meetings of his commission the same powers and duties as the Chairman of the Conference has in relation to plenary meetings. In the absence of the chairman, one of the vice-chairmen of the commission shall preside, with the same powers and duties.

5. The procedure in a commission shall be governed by the provisions of Rule XII, so far as applicable. One third of the members of a commission shall constitute a quorum for the consideration of items on the agenda of the commission and for decisions on questions of procedure with the exception of a motion for the closure of the debate on the item under discussion. A majority of the members of a commission shall constitute a quorum for decisions on substantive questions and for a decision on a motion for the closure of the debate on the item under discussion.

6. Meetings of commissions shall be held in public, unless the commission concerned decides otherwise.

7. Subject to any decision of the commission, the Director-General shall make arrangements for the admission of the public and of representatives of the press and other information agencies to meetings of commissions.

Rule XIV

Committees of commissions

1. Any commission may set up such committees as it considers necessary. Delegates of Associate Members shall have the right to participate in the deliberations of these committees, but shall not hold office or have the right to vote.

2. The chairman and members of each such committee shall be appointed by the commission concerned, upon the recommendation of its chairman. A member of a committee who is unable to be present at any meeting may be represented by another member of his delegation.

3. The chairman of each such committee shall have in relation to meetings of his committee the same powers and duties as the Chairman of the Conference has in relation to meetings of the Conference.

4. A majority of the members of each such committee shall constitute a quorum. Decisions in each such committee shall be taken by a majority of the votes cast. No member of any such committee shall have more than one vote.

5. Meetings of such committees shall be held in private unless otherwise determined by the appropriate commission.

Rule XV

Other committees of the Conference

1. The Conference may appoint, or authorize the appointment of, any temporary or special committee which it deems necessary. Delegates of Associate Members shall have the right to participate in the deliberations of any such committee, but shall not hold office or have the right to vote.

2. The chairman of any committee set up under this Rule shall be elected by such committee. He shall have, in relation to meetings of the committee, the same power and duties as the Chairman of the Conference has in relation to meetings of the Conference. A majority of the members of the committee shall constitute a quorum. Decisions in the committee shall be

taken by a majority of the votes cast. No member shall have more than one vote. A member of the committee who is unable to be present at any meeting may be represented by another member of his delegation. Meetings of the committee shall be held in private, unless otherwise determined by the Conference.

Rule XVI

Rapporteurs

1. The Conference or any commission or committee referred to in Rules XIII, XIV and XV above may appoint from among the delegations to the Conference one or more rapporteurs to carry out a preliminary study of a specific item and to submit their suggestions or conclusions to the Conference, commission or committee, as the case may be.

2. The Council, or its Chairman between sessions of the Council, may likewise appoint one or more rapporteurs from among the representatives of Members of the Council.

Rule XVII

Participating international organizations

1. A representative of the United Nations and a representative of any specialized agency of the United Nations, accompanied by advisers and assistants, may attend the plenary meetings of the Conference and the meetings of any commission, of any committee of a commission, and of any committee established under Rule XV. Such representatives may, without vote, speak and participate in the discussions and may circulate to the Conference, without abridgement, the views of the organizations which they represent.

2. An observer of any other intergovernmental organization with which an agreement has been concluded providing for representation, accompanied by advisers and assistants, may attend the plenary meetings of the Conference, and the meetings of any commission, of any technical committee of a commission and of any technical committee established under Rule XV. Such

observer may, without vote, speak and, upon the request of the Chairman, participate in the discussions. They may circulate to the Conference, without abridgement, the views of the organizations which they represent.

3. An observer of any international non-governmental organization having consultative status, accompanied by advisers and assistants, may attend the plenary meetings of the Conference and the meetings of any commission, of any technical committee of a commission and of any technical committee established under Rule XV. Such observers may, without vote, speak before such commissions and committees, participate in the discussions therein upon the request of the Chairman and, with the consent of the General Committee, speak before plenary meetings of the Conference. They may circulate to the Conference, without abridgement, the views of the organizations which they represent.

4. The Director-General shall determine provisionally what other international organizations shall be invited to any session of the Conference and shall submit the list of such organizations to the Conference for approval.

Rule XVIII

Records and reports

1. Verbatim records shall be kept for all plenary and commission meetings. Unless otherwise expressly decided by the committee concerned, no record shall be kept of the proceedings of the General Committee, the Nominations Committee, the Credentials Committee, any committee of a commission, or any committee established under Rule XV, other than the reports presented to the Conference.

2. The verbatim records and reports referred to in paragraph 1 shall be circulated as soon as possible to delegations attending the Conference in order to give members of delegations who participated in the meeting concerned the opportunity to check the accuracy of the record of their interventions.

3. As soon as possible after the end of the session, copies of all verbatim records and a report embodying all resolutions, recommendations, conventions, agreements, and other formal decisions adopted or approved by the Con-

ference shall be transmitted by the Director-General to all Member Nations and Associate Members.

Rule XIX

Admission of additional Member Nations and Associate Members

1. Any nation or regional economic integration organization which desires to become a Member of the Organization and any Member Nation or authority which wishes to request admission to associate membership on behalf of a territory or a group of territories for whose international relations it is responsible shall submit an application to the Director-General. This application shall be accompanied or followed by the formal instrument of acceptance of the Constitution, required under Article II, paragraph 2 or 3 of the Constitution. This formal instrument shall reach the Director-General not later than the opening day of the Conference session at which the admission of the applicant is to be considered.

2. Any such application shall be transmitted immediately by the Director-General to Member Nations and shall be placed on the agenda of the next Conference session which opens not less than 30 days from the receipt of the application.

3. The first contribution of an additional Member Nation or Associate Member shall be determined by the Conference at the time of its decision on the application for membership.

4. The Director-General shall inform the applicant nation or regional economic integration organization of the decision of the Conference. If the application is approved, such notice shall also state the amount of the first contribution.

Rule XX

Budget and finance

The Conference shall, at each regular session:

(*a*) examine and adopt the budget for the ensuing financial period;

(*b*) adopt the final accounts of the Organization for the preceding financial period, after having considered the report of the Council thereon;

(*c*) consider the report of the Director-General on the receipt of contributions from Member Nations and Associate Members since the previous session; and

(*d*) on the recommendation of the Council, or on the request of a Member Nation transmitted to the Director-General not later than 120 days before the opening of the session, re-examine the scale of contributions of Member Nations.

Rule XXI

Conventions and agreements

1. (*a*) To secure proper consultation pursuant to paragraph 6 of Article XIV of the Constitution, the Director-General shall notify Member Nations and Associate Members of any proposal for a convention, agreement, supplementary convention or agreement under Article XIV of the Constitution, not later than the time when he dispatches the agenda of the session of the Conference or Council at which the matter is to be considered. Such notification shall be accompanied by:

   (*i*) any reports on the matter by the Director-General, including a report on the technical, administrative and financial implications, if any, of such convention, agreement, supplementary convention or agreement; and

   (*ii*) a request for comments and information on the matter and for such representations as Member Nations or Associate Members may wish to make.

(*b*) The Director-General shall, at the same time as he is requesting Member Nations and Associate Members for their comments on the proposed convention, agreement, supplementary convention or agreement, consult the United Nations and other specialized agencies and, at his discretion, other international organizations in respect of any provision of the proposed convention, agreement, supplementary convention or agreement which relates to the activities of such organizations or agencies.

(*c*) The Conference or the Council, after having considered any representations that may have been made to it or comments submitted by Member

Nations and Associate Members, and any comments from the United Nations, any specialized agency, or other international organization, may approve only such conventions, agreements, supplementary conventions or agreements as contain provisions to the effect that:

(*i*) any international body or machinery to be set up or any activity to be undertaken under such convention, agreement, supplementary convention or agreement is within the framework of the Organization;

(*ii*) recommendations adopted and reports on activities carried out by any such body shall be transmitted to the Director-General of the Organization.

2. The Council shall report to the Conference any action it takes under paragraph 2 of Article XIV of the Constitution.

3. The receipt of the official text of a convention, agreement, supplementary convention or agreement, as approved by the Conference or Council, shall constitute due notice to each Member Nation concerned, and to the authority having responsibility for the international relations of an Associate Member, that its consideration thereof is invited with a view to acceptance. Each Member Nation accepting shall communicate its acceptance to the Director-General, who shall promptly inform the other Member Nations.

4. The full powers given to a government representative to sign a convention, agreement, supplementary convention or agreement should be issued by the authority endowed with the inherent power to bind the state, such as the government, the head of the state, the head of the government, the minister of foreign affairs or the minister of the department concerned. Instruments of accession or of acceptance should likewise be issued by one of these authorities. When speedy action is required, signature, accession or acceptance may be effected by the delegate of the government concerned or the head of its diplomatic mission in the country where the signature, accession or acceptance is to take place, subject to the deposit with the Director-General of a written statement issued by the head of the diplomatic mission certifying that such action is being taken in accordance with full powers conferred by the government and that the necessary formal instrument will be forthcoming.

5. The Director-General shall report to the Conference whenever a convention, agreement, supplementary convention or agreement has, in accor-

dance with its terms, come into force or ceased to be in force, or has been amended and the amendments come into force.

B. THE COUNCIL

Rule XXII

Election of the Council

1. (*a*) Except as provided in paragraph 9 of this Rule, the Council shall be elected for a term of three years.

(*b*) The Conference shall make such provisions as will ensure that the terms of office of sixteen Members of the Council shall expire in each of two successive calendar years and seventeen in the third calendar year.

(*c*) The terms of office of all members of any one group shall expire simultaneously either on the termination of the regular session of the Conference in a year in which such a session is held, or on 31 December in other years.

2. The Conference shall, at each regular session, and after considering any recommendations of the General Committee, fill all vacancies due to the expiration of the terms of office of Council Members at the end of that session or at the end of the following year, in conformity with the provisions of the preceding paragraph.

3. In selecting Members of the Council, the Conference shall give due consideration to the desirability of:

(*a*) including in its membership a balanced geographical representation of nations interested in the production, distribution and consumption of food and agricultural products;

(*b*) ensuring the participation in the work of the Council of such Member Nations as contribute in a large measure towards the success of the Organization;

(*c*) giving to the greatest possible number of Member Nations an opportunity, by rotation of membership, to serve on the Council.

4. Member Nations shall be eligible for re-election.

5. No Member Nation shall be eligible for election to the Council if it is in arrears in payment of its financial contributions to the Organization in an amount equal to or exceeding the contributions due from it for the two preceding calendar years.

6. The Conference shall, at any regular or special session, fill all other vacancies on the Council which may have occurred since the last regular session. In the case of a special session, the General Committee shall recommend to the Conference such readjustments as circumstances may warrant to the time limits provided for in paragraph 10 (*a*) and (*d*) below.

7. A Member of the Council shall be considered to have resigned if it is in arrears in payment of its financial contributions to the Organization in an amount equal to or exceeding the contributions due from it for the two preceding calendar years, or if it has not been represented at two consecutive sessions of the Council.

8. Any Member Nation on the Council that withdraws from the Organization shall cease to be a Member of the Council when its notice of withdrawal from the Organization takes effect under Article XIX of the Constitution.

9. The term of office of a member elected to take the place of a member who has resigned or withdrawn from the Council before the expiration of its term of office shall be for the remainder of the term of office of the member replaced.

10. In addition to the relevant provisions of Rule XII governing election procedure, the following provisions of this paragraph shall apply:

(*a*) As soon as possible after the opening of the Conference session, and in any case before the end of the third day of the session, the Conference, on the recommendation of its General Committee, shall decide the date of the election and the date by which nominations for election to the Council must be submitted, in accordance with subparagraph (*c*) below.

(*b*) Each nomination shall be made for a specific region as determined by the Conference, indicating the term of office to which it applies, subject to the provisions of subparagraph (*g*) of this paragraph. No nomination shall be made for a term that includes a period for which the Member Nation concerned is already in office.

(*c*) Each nomination shall be supported, in writing, by the delegates of two Member Nations to the Conference other than the delegate of the Member Nation nominated and shall be accompanied by a formal written acceptance of the nomination by the delegate of the Member Nation nominated. Any nomination reaching the Secretary General of the Conference and Council after the date and time determined by the Conference for the submission of nominations shall not be valid.

(*d*) The General Committee shall, at least three working days before the date selected for the election, communicate to the Conference in English alphabetical order the valid nominations received for each region and term of office, formally drawing the attention of the Conference to the provisions of paragraphs 3 and 4 of this Rule. The names of the nominators shall not be communicated by the General Committee to the Conference.

(*e*) Before submitting the nominations to the Conference, the General Committee shall ensure that the conditions regarding eligibility contained in paragraph 5 of this Rule are fulfilled.

(*f*) The General Committee may submit recommendations to the Conference on any other aspect of the election.

(*g*) The election of Council Members shall be conducted in accordance with the provisions of paragraphs 9 (*b*) and 12 of Rule XII, one election being held to fill simultaneously all the vacancies occurring in each region in each of the calendar years referred to in paragraph 1 of this Rule. Should the number of Member Nations standing for election in a particular region be equal to the total number of vacancies occurring in both calendar years, one election may be held to fill simultaneously all these vacancies, and the allocation of candidates to the vacancies occurring in each year may be settled, where necessary, by mutual agreement or by the Conference by such methods as it may decide to adopt. Candidates who are unsuccessful in the election to fill the vacancy or vacancies occurring in the first calendar year shall be included among the candidates for election to the vacancy or vacancies occurring at the end of the second calendar year, except where they voluntarily withdraw.

Rule XXIII

Chairman of the Council

1. In pursuance of paragraph 2 of Article V of the Constitution, the Conference shall appoint an independent Chairman of the Council under the following conditions:

(*a*) The Chairman of the Council shall be appointed for a term of office of two years which shall be renewable for the same period after which it shall not be renewable.

(*b*) The appointment of the Chairman of the Council shall be placed on the agenda of each regular session of the Conference. Nominations validly made in accordance with Rule XII.5 of these Rules shall be communicated to the Secretary-General of the Conference and Council by the date set by the Council. The Secretary-General shall circulate these nominations to all Member Governments and Associate Members by the date likewise set by the Council. As soon as possible after the opening of the Conference session, the General Committee shall determine and announce the date of the election.

(*c*) The conditions of appointment of the Chairman of the Council, including the allowances attached to the office, shall be determined by the Conference on the occasion of each appointment, having regard to any recommendations of the General Committee.

2. The Chairman of the Council shall have no vote.

3. If the independent Chairman of the Council is prevented from exercising his functions for the remainder of his term of office due to resignation, disability, death or for any other reason, his functions shall *ipso facto* be assumed by the Chairman of the Programme Committee for the remainder of the term of office. The Director-General shall forthwith notify all Member Nations and Associate Members and the Chairman of the Programme Committee thereof.

4. The Chairman of the Programme Committee shall receive on a *pro rata* basis for such period as he may be called upon to act as Chairman of the Council such emoluments as were approved by the Conference when determining the conditions of appointment of the Chairman of the Council whom he succeeds.

Rule XXIV

Functions of the Council

The Council, subject to the provisions of paragraph 3 of Article V of the Constitution, shall, between sessions of the Conference, act on behalf of the Conference as its executive organ and make decisions on matters that need not be submitted to the Conference. In particular, the Council shall exercise the functions described below:

1. *World food and agriculture situation and related matters*

The Council shall:

(*a*) keep under review the state of food and agriculture in the world, and consider the programmes of Member Nations and Associate Members;

(*b*) tender advice on such matters to governments of Member Nations and Associate Members, intergovernmental commodity councils or other commodity authorities and through the Director-General to other specialized international agencies;

(*c*) draw up a provisional agenda for the review by the Conference of the state of food and agriculture, drawing attention to specific policy issues which would require Conference consideration or could be the subject of a formal recommendation by the Conference under paragraph 3 of Article IV of the Constitution, and aid the Director-General to prepare the report and agenda for the review by the Conference of the programmes of Member Nations and Associate Members;

(*d*) (*i*) examine current developments in proposed and existing intergovernmental agricultural commodity arrangements, particularly those developments affecting adequacy of food supply, utilization of food reserves and famine relief, changes in production or pricing policies and special food programmes for undernourished groups;

(*ii*) promote consistency and integration of agricultural commodity policies, national and international, with regard to (*a*) overall objectives of the Organization; (*b*) the interrelationships of production, distribution and consumption; and (*c*) interrelationships of agricultural commodities;

(*iii*) initiate and authorize groups to study and investigate agricultural commodity situations which are becoming critical, and propose appropriate action, if necessary, under paragraph 2 (*f*) of Article I of the Constitution;

(*iv*) advise on emergency measures such as those relating to the export and import of food and materials or equipment needed for agricultural production, in order to facilitate implementation of national programmes and, if necessary, request the Director-General to submit such advice for action to the Member Nations and Associate Members concerned;

(*v*) perform the foregoing functions under (*i*), (*ii*) and (*iii*) in conformity with the Economic and Social Council's Resolution of 28 March 1947[1] relating to international commodity arrangements, and generally act in close cooperation with the appropriate specialized agencies and intergovernmental bodies.

---

[1] RESOLUTION 30 (IV) OF THE FOURTH SESSION OF THE ECONOMIC AND SOCIAL COUNCIL
Adopted on 28 March 1947
THE ECONOMIC AND SOCIAL COUNCIL,

NOTING that intergovernmental consultations are going forward actively with respect to certain internationally traded commodities, and

CONSIDERING the significant measure of agreement regarding commodity problems and the coordination of commodity consultations already reached both in the first session of the Preparatory Committee of the United Nations Conference on Trade and Employment, and in the Preparatory Commission on World Food Proposals of the Food and Agriculture Organization of the United Nations,*

RECOMMENDS that, pending the establishment of the International Trade Organization, members of the United Nations adopt as a general guide in intergovernmental consultation or action with respect to commodity problems, the principles laid down in Chapter VII as a whole, i.e., the chapter on intergovernmental commodity arrangements of the draft charter appended to the report of the first session of the Preparatory Committee of the United Nations Conference on Trade and Employment, although recognizing that discussions in future sessions of the Preparatory Committee of the United Nations Conference, as well as in the Conference itself, may result in modifications of the provisions relating to commodity problems; and

REQUESTS the Secretary-General to appoint an interim coordinating committee for international commodity arrangements, to keep informed of and to facilitate by appropriate means such intergovernmental consultation or action with respect to commodity problems, the committee to consist of a chairman to represent the Preparatory Committee of the United Nations Conference on Trade and Employment, a person nominated by the Food and Agriculture Organization of the United Nations to be concerned in particular with agricultural primary commodities, and a person to be concerned in particular with nonagricultural primary commodities.

---

* See report of the first session of the Preparatory Committee of the United Nations Conference on Trade and Employment (document E/PC/T/33, published as a working document only) and report of the Preparatory Commission on World Food Proposals of the Food and Agriculture Organization of the United Nations.

2. *Current and prospective activities of the Organization, including its Programme of Work and Budget*

The Council shall:

(*a*) consider, and make recommendations to the Conference on, policy issues regarding:

(*i*) the summary and draft Programme of Work and Budget and supplementary estimates submitted by the Director-General for the following financial period;

(*ii*) the activities of the Organization in connection with the United Nations Development Programme;

(*b*) take any necessary action, within the approved Programme of Work and Budget, with respect to the technical activities of the Organization and report to the Conference on such policy aspects thereof as may require decisions by the Conference.

3. *Administrative matters and financial management of the Organization*

The Council shall:

(*a*) exercise control over the financial administration of the Organization;

(*b*) report to the Conference on the financial position and the final audited accounts of the Organization;

(*c*) advise the Director-General on matters of policy affecting administration;

(*d*) approve between-chapter transfers other than those for which the Finance Committee has authority;

(*e*) authorize withdrawals from the Working Capital Fund for making reimbursable loans or for emergency expenditure on the basis of proposals from the Director-General;

(*f*) consider and make recommendations to the Conference on the level of the Working Capital Fund;

(*g*) consider the establishment of reserve funds and make recommendations thereon to the Conference;

(*h*) consider and make recommendations to the Conference on any proposal from the Director-General to accept voluntary contributions and to establish Trust and Special Funds involving additional financial obligations for Member Nations and Associate Members;

(*i*) consider the scale of contributions and recommend any modifications thereof to the Conference;

(*j*) consider and approve recommendations of the Finance Committee or the International Civil Service Commission regarding the scale of salaries and the conditions of employment of the staff and recommendations of the Finance Committee on the general structure of the administrative and technical services of the Organization;

(*k*) consider any observations of the Finance Committee on decisions taken by the International Civil Service Commission in accordance with its Statute, including the funding of post adjustments applied to salary rates;

(*l*) review action by the Director-General in regard to new posts established in the professional category of staff for which prior authority did not exist;

(*m*) appoint the external auditor;

(*n*) delegate to the Finance Committee specific functions relating to financial or administrative matters of the Organization in addition to the functions listed in Rule XXVII, paragraph 7 of these Rules.

4. *Constitutional matters*

The Council may:

(*a*) establish commissions, committees and working parties, and convene general, regional, technical or other conferences, working parties or consultations, or authorize the Director-General to establish committees and working parties and convene general, regional, technical or other conferences, working parties or consultations, pursuant to Article VI of the Constitution;

(*b*) consider, and approve for submission to Member Nations, agreements and supplementary conventions or agreements, as provided in paragraph 2 of Article XIV of the Constitution;

(*c*) subject to confirmation by the Conference, enter into agreements with other international organizations, pursuant to paragraph 1 of Article XIII of the Constitution;

(*d*) make recommendations concerning the relationship between the Organization and international non-governmental organizations, in accordance with procedures determined by the Conference;

(*e*) consider, and make recommendations to the Conference on amendments to the General Rules and the Financial Regulations of the Organization.

5. *General*

The Council shall:

(*a*) elect the Chairmen and Members of the Programme Committee and the Finance Committee, and the Members of the Committee on Constitutional and Legal Matters;

(*b*) propose candidates for the office of Chairman of the Conference, the chairmen of the commissions of the Conference, the three Vice-Chairmen of the Conference, the Members of the Credentials Committee and the elected Members of the General Committee;

(*c*) recommend, after consultation with the Director-General, items for insertion in the agenda of any session of the Conference which require consideration by the Conference, supervise and coordinate all preparatory work for Conference sessions, keeping in mind the desirability of confining, as far as possible, the provisional agenda of these sessions to major policy issues;

(*d*) advise the Director-General on matters of policy and exercise the general supervision provided for in Rule XXXVII, paragraph 1;

(*e*) perform such other functions as are necessary to assist in the effective functioning of the Organization;

(*f*) report to the Conference on its work, emphasizing policy issues for consideration by the Conference.

Rule XXV

Sessions of the Council

1. The Council shall hold a session as often as it considers necessary or on the call of its Chairman or the Director-General, or on request submitted in writing to the Director-General by five or more Member Nations.

2. The Council shall in any event hold three sessions between the regular sessions of the Conference, as follows:

(*a*) one session immediately after the regular session of the Conference;

(*b*) one session in the first year of the biennium approximately midway between the regular sessions of the Conference; and (*c*) one session not less than 120 days before the regular session of the Conference.

3. At its session held immediately after a regular session of the Conference the Council shall:

(*a*) elect the Chairmen and Members of the Programme Committee and the Finance Committee, and the Members of the Committee on Constitutional and Legal Matters;

(*b*) take any action of an urgent nature arising out of decisions of the Conference.

4. At its session held in the first year of the biennium, approximately midway between the regular sessions of the Conference, the Council shall in particular conduct on behalf of the Conference a world review of the state of food and agriculture and exercise the function provided in paragraph 1 (*b*) of Rule XXIV of these Rules.

5. At its session held in the second year of the biennium, not less than 120 days prior to the regular session of the Conference, the Council shall in particular exercise the functions provided in paragraphs 1 (*c*), 2 (*a*) and, insofar as possible, those provided in paragraph 5 (*b*) of Rule XXIV of these Rules.

6. The travelling expenses of not more than one member of the delegation of each Member Nation on the Council, properly incurred in travelling, by the most direct route, from the member's capital city or duty station, whichever is less, to the site of the Council's session and return to his or her capital city or duty station, shall be borne by the Organization.

7. (*a*) The Director-General, in consultation with the Chairman of the Council, and having regard to suggestions made by any Member Nation or Associate Member acting within the limits of its status, shall prepare a provisional agenda and dispatch it to Member Nations and Associate Members by airmail not less than 60 days in advance of the session. Documentation shall be circulated with the provisional agenda or as soon as possible thereafter.

(*b*) Any Member of the Council may request the Director-General, not less than 30 days before the proposed date of any session, to insert an item in the provisional agenda for that session. The Director-General shall thereupon, if necessary, circulate a revised provisional agenda to all Member Nations and Associate Members, together with any necessary papers.

(*c*) During any session, the Council may, by a vote concurred in by at least two thirds of the membership of the Council, add to the agenda any item proposed by a Member of the Council.

8. Subject to any decisions of the Conference and to any agreements between the Organization and other organizations, the Council may arrange for consultation with the United Nations, with any specialized agency of the United Nations, and with such other international organizations as it deems to be appropriate, and for their participation, without vote, in its discussions.

9. (*a*) Subject to the provisions of subparagraphs (*b*) and (*c*) below, meetings of the Council and of such of its committees as are open to all of its members shall be public.

(*b*) The Council may decide to meet in private for the discussion of any particular item on its agenda.

(*c*) Any Member Nation not represented on the Council and any Associate Member may submit memoranda on any item on the agenda of the Council and participate without vote in any discussion at a public or private meeting of the Council or of such of its committees as are open to all of its Members, unless, in exceptional circumstances, the Council decides that it is necessary in the interests of the Organization to restrict attendance to the representative of each Member of the Council.

10. The Council may set up at each of its sessions and for the duration of the session such committees as it considers desirable and allocate to these committees the various items on its agenda. The Council may also establish ad hoc committees consisting of a limited number of Council Members, to meet between Council sessions for the purpose of examining, and reporting on, such questions as the Council may have referred to them.

11. The Council may make arrangements for participation by observers from non-member nations in discussions on particular items of the Council agenda, in appropriate meetings of the Council or its committees, and for the submission of memoranda.

12. The Council shall make provision for keeping all Member Nations and Associate Members of the Organization informed of its activities.

13. The Director-General or his representative shall attend all meetings of the Council.

14. Should matters of exceptional urgency arise between two sessions of the Council, on which Council action is required, the Director-General, after having consulted the Chairman of the Council, or after notifying him, should such consultation not prove feasible, may seek the opinion of the Members of the Council by any rapid means of communication, informing at the same time all other Member Nations as well as Associate Members and the Chairman of the Council. Subject to the provisions of paragraph 1 of this Rule, the Director-General may proceed with the action contemplated as soon as he has received concurrence by cable or letter either from the majority of the Members of the Council in cases where decisions of the Council normally have to be taken by a majority of the votes cast, or from two thirds of the Members of the Council where a qualified majority is required. Any such action shall be immediately reported by the Director-General to all Member Nations and Associate Members of the Organization and to the Chairman of the Council.

Rule XXVI

Programme Committee

1. The Programme Committee provided for in paragraph 6 of Article V of the Constitution shall be composed of representatives of eleven Member Nations of the Organization. Such Member Nations shall be elected by the Council in accordance with the procedure set forth in paragraph 3 of this Rule. Members of the Committee shall appoint as their representatives individuals who have shown a continued interest in the objectives and activities of the Organization, have participated in Conference or Council sessions and have special competence and experience in economic, social and technical matters pertaining to the various fields of the Organization's activities. Members of the Committee shall be elected for a period of two years at the session of the Council immediately following the regular session of the Conference. They shall be eligible for reappointment.

2. A Member Nation of the Organization seeking election as a member of the Committee shall, as soon as possible but not later than ten days before the opening date of the Council session at which the election is to be held, communicate to the Secretary-General of the Conference and Council the name of the representative that it would appoint if elected and details of his qualifications and experience. The Secretary-General of the Conference and Council shall circulate this information in writing to Members of the Council before the Council session at which the election is to be held.

3. The following procedures shall apply to the election of Members of the Committee:

(*a*) Member Nations shall present their candidature for election in respect of a specific region as determined by the Conference for the purpose of Council elections.

(*b*) The Council shall first elect a Chairman from among the designated representatives of the prospective Members of the Committee.

(*c*) After the election referred to in subparagraph (*b*) above, the Council shall proceed to the election of the other Members of the Committee, in two stages, making the necessary adjustment to take into account the Member Nation of which the Chairman is a national and the region to which that Member Nation belongs:

(*i*) the first stage shall be to elect eight Members from the following regions: Africa, Asia and the Pacific, Near East, and Latin America and the Caribbean;

(*ii*) the second stage shall be to elect three Members from the following regions: Europe, North America, and Southwest Pacific.

(*d*) Except as provided in subparagraph (*b*) above, the election of Members of the Committee shall be conducted in accordance with the provisions of paragraphs 8 (*b*) and 13 of Rule XII of these Rules, one election being held to fill simultaneously all the vacancies occurring in each group of regions specified in subparagraph (*e*) above.

(e) The other provisions on voting arrangements in Rule XII of these Rules shall apply *mutatis mutandis* to the election of Members of the Committee.

4. (*a*) If the representative of a Member of the Committee is expected to be unable to attend a session of the Committee, or if, due to incapacity, death or any other reason he is prevented from exercising his functions for the remainder of the term for which the Member he represents has been elected, that Member shall inform the Director-General and the Chairman as soon as possible, and may designate a substitute representative who shall have the qualifications and experience referred to in paragraph 1 of this Rule. The Council shall be informed of the qualifications and experience of the substitute representative.

(*b*) The provisions of subparagraph (*a*) shall also apply to the Chairman of the Committee except that, in the absence of the Chairman elected by the Council, his functions shall be exercised by the Vice-Chairman elected in accordance with the Rules of Procedure of the Committee.

5. The Chairman of the Programme Committee may attend sessions of the Conference or Council when the report of the Programme Committee is considered.

6. The Chairman of the Council may attend all meetings of the Programme Committee.

7. The Programme Committee shall have the following functions:

(*a*) to review:

(*i*) the current activities of the Organization;

(*ii*) the summary and draft Programme of Work and Budget of the Organization for the ensuing biennium, particularly with respect to:

- content and balance of the programme, having regard to the extent to which it is proposed that existing activities be expanded, reduced in scope or discontinued;
- the extent of coordination of work between the different technical divisions of the Organization and between the Organization and other international organizations;
- the priorities to be given to existing activities, extension of such activities and to new activities;

(*iii*) the programme aspects of the United Nations Development Programme with which the Organization is concerned;

(*b*) to consider the matters listed in Rule XXVIII of these Rules;

(*c*) to advise the Council on the long-term programme objectives of the Organization;

(*d*) to adopt and amend its own rules of procedure, which shall be consistent with the Constitution and the General Rules of the Organization;

(*e*) to consider any other matter submitted to it by the Council or the Director-General;

(*f*) to report to the Council or tender advice to the Director-General, as appropriate, on matters considered by the Committee.

8. The Programme Committee shall hold sessions on the call of its Chairman or of the Director-General. It shall, in any event, hold one session annually.

9. Representatives of Members of the Committee shall be reimbursed for the cost of their travel expenses, properly incurred in travelling, by the most direct route, from their duty station to the site of the Committee session and return to their duty station. They shall also be paid a subsistence allowance while attending sessions of the Committee, in accordance with the travel regulations of the Organization.

Rule XXVII

Finance Committee

1. The Finance Committee provided for in paragraph 6 of Article V of the Constitution shall be composed of representatives of nine Member Nations of the Organization. Such Member Nations shall be elected by the Council in accordance with the procedure set forth in paragraph 3 of this Rule. Members of the Committee shall appoint as their representatives individuals who have shown a continued interest in the objectives and activities of the Organization, have participated in Conference or Council sessions and have special competence and experience in administrative and financial matters. Members of the Committee shall be elected for a period of two years at the session of the Council immediately following the regular session of the Conference. They shall be eligible for reappointment.

2. A Member Nation of the Organization seeking election as a Member of the Committee shall, as soon as possible but not later than ten days before the opening date of the Council session at which the election is to be held, communicate to the Secretary-General of the Conference and Council the name of the representative that it would appoint if elected and details of his qualifications and experience. The Secretary-General of the Conference and Council shall circulate this information in writing to Members of the Council before the Council session at which the election is to be held.

3. The following procedures shall apply to the election of Members of the Committee:

(*a*) Member Nations shall present their candidature for election in respect of a specific region as determined by the Conference for the purpose of Council elections.

(*b*) The Council shall first elect a Chairman from among the designated representatives of the prospective Members of the Committee.

(*c*) After the election referred to in subparagraph (*b*) above, the Council shall proceed to the election of the other Members of the Committee, in two stages, making the necessary adjustment to take into account the Member Nation of which the Chairman is a national and the region to which that Member Nation belongs:

(*i*) the first stage shall be to elect six Members from the following regions: Africa, Asia and the Pacific, Near East, and Latin America and the Caribbean;

(*ii*) the second stage shall be to elect three Members from the following regions: Europe, North America, and Southwest Pacific.

(*d*) Except as provided in subparagraph (*b*) above, the election of Members of the Committee shall be conducted in accordance with the provisions of paragraphs 9 (*b*) and 13 of Rule XII of these Rules, one election being held to fill simultaneously all the vacancies occurring in each group of regions specified in subparagraph (*c*) above.

(*e*) The other provisions on voting arrangements in Rule XII of these Rules shall apply *mutatis mutandis* to the election of Members of the Committee.

4. (*a*) If the representative of a Member of the Committee is expected to be unable to attend a session of the Committee, or if, due to incapacity, death or any other reason, he is prevented from exercising his functions for the remainder of the term for which the Member he represents has been elected, that Member shall inform the Director-General and the Chairman as soon as possible, and may designate a substitute representative who shall have the qualifications and experience referred to in paragraph 1 of this Rule. The Council shall be informed of the qualifications and experience of the substitute representative.

(*b*) The provisions of subparagraph (*a*) shall also apply to the Chairman of the Committee except that, in the absence of the Chairman elected by the Council, his functions shall be exercised by the Vice-Chairman elected in accordance with the Rules of Procedure of the Committee.

5. The Chairman of the Finance Committee may attend sessions of the Council or Conference when the report of the Finance Committee is considered.

6. The Chairman of the Council may attend all meetings of the Finance Committee.

7. The Finance Committee shall assist the Council in exercising control over the financial administration of the Organization and shall have, in particular, the following functions:

(*a*) to review the financial implications of the Director-General's budgetary proposals, including proposals for supplementary estimates, and to make recommendations thereon to the Council regarding important matters;

(*b*) to examine the Director-General's proposals with regard to the acceptance of voluntary contributions which involve additional financial obligations for Member Nations or Associate Members, and to submit recommendations thereon to the Council;

(*c*) to review the reports submitted by the Director-General in accordance with Financial Regulation 4.5 (*a*);

(*d*) to approve budgetary transfers proposed by the Director-General under the terms of Financial Regulation 4.5 (*b*) (*i*); and to review proposals of the Director-General regarding budgetary transfers under the terms of Financial Regulation 4.5 (*b*) (*ii*), making recommendations thereon to the Council;

(*e*) to inform the Programme Committee of any budgetary transfers that may have significant programme implications;

(*f*) to review the Director-General's proposals to make withdrawals from the Working Capital Fund for emergency expenditure or reimbursable loans and make recommendations thereon to the Council;

(*g*) to consider, and make recommendations to the Council on the establishment of reserve funds;

(*h*) to review the reports of the Director-General on the establishment of Trust and Special Funds, and to make recommendations to the Council regarding such funds as involve additional financial obligations for Member Nations and Associate Members;

(*i*) to consider reports on investments submitted by the Director-General in accordance with Financial Regulation 9.2, and to keep the Organization's investment policy under review;

(*j*) to keep under review the scale of contributions and to submit recommendations to the Council regarding any modification of such scale;

(*k*) to consider the reports of the Director-General on *ex gratia* payments;

(*l*) to examine, on behalf of the Council, the audited accounts of the Organization, to review, in consultation with the Director-General, reports on the current financial position of the Organization submitted by the Director-General, and to report to the Council on these matters;

(*m*) to recommend to the Council the appointment of the external auditor;

(*n*) to determine, after consultation with the external auditor, the scope of the audit;

(*o*) to examine the report of the external auditor and to report to the Council on matters involving policy issues;

(*p*) to consider and/or recommend proposals for the amendment of the Financial Regulations of the Organization and to submit recommendations to the Council for transmission to the Conference;

(*q*) to keep under review, and consider any amendments to, the detailed financial rules and procedures referred to in Financial Regulation 10.1 (*a*);

(*r*) to consider proposals of the Director-General and recommendations of the International Civil Service Commission on the scale of salaries and conditions of employment of the staff and proposals of the Director-General on the general structure of the administrative and technical services of the Organization;

(*s*) to consider reports by the Director-General on decisions taken by the International Civil Service Commission in accordance with its Statute, including the funding of post adjustments applied to salary rates, and to submit any observations thereon to the Council;

(*t*) to adopt and amend its own Rules of Procedure, which shall be consistent with the Constitution and the General Rules of the Organization;

(*u*) to perform such other functions relating to financial or administrative matters of the Organization as may be provided for in these Rules and the Financial Regulations, and to perform such other duties as may be referred to it by the Council;

(*v*) to consider the matters listed in Rule XXVIII of these Rules.

8. The Finance Committee shall hold sessions as often as necessary, either:

(*a*) on the call of its Chairman acting on his own initiative or in pursuance of a decision of the Committee or of a request submitted in writing to the Chairman by three Members of the Committee; or

(*b*) on the call of the Director-General acting on his own initiative or in pursuance of a request submitted in writing to him by five or more Member Nations.

The Finance Committee shall in any event hold one session annually. Additional sessions may be held to provide consultation on financial matters with the appropriate commissions of the Conference.

9. Representatives of Members of the Committee shall be reimbursed for the cost of their travel expenses, properly incurred in travelling, by the most direct route, from their duty station to the site of the Committee session and return to their duty station. They shall also be paid a subsistence allowance while attending sessions of the Committee, in accordance with the travel regulations of the Organization.

Rule XXVIII

Concurrent sessions and joint meetings of the Programme and Finance Committees

1. In the second year of the biennium, the Programme Committee and the Finance Committee shall hold concurrent sessions. At these sessions the two Committees shall, *inter alia*, review separately the summary and draft Programme of Work and Budget submitted by the Director-General for the following biennium. The Programme Committee shall consider the programme and relevant financial aspects of the summary and draft Programme of Work, while the Finance Committee shall consider the financial aspects of the summary and draft Programme of Work and Budget without concerning itself with the merits of the Programme.

2. Towards the end of the concurrent sessions mentioned above, the two Committees shall hold joint meetings to consider:

(*a*) the financial implications of the technical aspects of the summary and draft Programme of Work;

(*b*) the implications of the summary and draft Programme of Work insofar as the level of the budget is concerned;

(*c*) the financial implications with respect to future years of the activities provided for in the summary and draft Programme of Work and Budget;

(*d*) the format to be adopted for the presentation of the summary and draft Programme of Work and Budget in order to facilitate the review thereof;

(*e*) any other matters of joint interest to the two Committees which fall within their terms of reference.

3. The Programme and Finance Committees shall submit to the Council a consolidated report on such aspects of the summary and draft Programme of Work and Budget as are of joint interest, setting out the main features thereof and emphasizing policy issues for consideration by the Council or the Conference.

Rule XXIX

Committee on Commodity Problems

1. The Committee on Commodity Problems provided for in paragraph 6 of Article V of the Constitution shall be open to all Member Nations of the Organization. It shall be composed of those Member Nations which notify the Director-General in writing of their desire to become Members of the Committee and of their intention to participate in the work of the Committee.

2. The notifications referred to in paragraph 1 may be made at any time and membership acquired on the basis thereof shall be for a biennium. The Director-General shall circulate, at the beginning of each session of the Committee, a document listing the Members of the Committee.

3. The Committee shall elect its own Chairman from among its Members.

4. The Committee shall normally hold two sessions during each biennium, to be convened by the Director-General in consultation with the Chairman of the Committee, taking into account any proposals made by the Committee. One of these sessions shall be convened sufficiently in advance of the session of the Council held approximately midway between the regular sessions of the Conference, in order that the report of the Committee may be circulated to the Members of the Council, in accordance with the provisions of Rule XXV.7 (*a*) of these Rules.

5. If required, the Committee may hold additional sessions on the call of its Chairman or the Director-General or on request submitted in writing to the Director-General by a majority of the Members of the Committee.

6. The Committee shall:

(*a*) keep under review commodity problems of an international character affecting production, trade, distribution, consumption and related economic matters;

(*b*) prepare a factual and interpretative survey of the world commodity situation, which may be made available directly to Member Nations;

(*c*) report and submit suggestions to the Council on policy issues arising out of its deliberations. The reports of the Committee and its subsidiary bodies shall be made available to Member Nations for their information.

7. The Committee shall take full account of the responsibilities and activities of the Committee on World Food Security and of the Committee on Food Aid Policies and Programmes in order to avoid overlapping and unnecessary duplication of work.

8. The Director-General or his representative shall participate in all meetings of the Committee and may be accompanied by such officers of the staff of the Organization as he may designate.

9. The Committee may adopt and amend its own Rules of Procedure, which shall be consistent with the Constitution and the General Rules of the Organization.

10. The Committee may, when necessary, establish subcommittees, intergovernmental commodity groups and ad hoc subsidiary bodies, subject to the necessary funds being available in the relevant chapter of the approved budget of the Organization. It may include in the membership of such subcommittees and ad hoc subsidiary bodies Member Nations which are not Members of the Committee and Associate Members. Membership of intergovernmental commodity groups established by the Committee shall be open to all Member Nations and Associate Members of the Organization, and the Council may admit to membership of such groups States which, while not Member Nations or Associate Members of the Organization, are members of the United Nations, any of its specialized agencies or the International Atomic Energy Agency. It may authorize the Director-General to invite at their request States which, while not Member Nations or Associate Members of the Organization, are members of the United Nations, any of its specialized agencies or the International Atomic Energy Agency, to attend consultations, convened under paragraph 1 (*d*) of Rule XXIV of the General Rules of the Organization, on individual commodities and participate in the discussions, with the right to vote and to hold office. Former Member Nations of the Organization which have withdrawn leaving arrears of contributions shall not be admitted to membership in intergovernmental commodity groups or attend consultations on individual commodities until such time as they have paid up all such arrears or the Confer-

ence has approved an arrangement for the settlement thereof, or unless the Council, in special circumstances, decides otherwise with respect to such admission.

11. The subsidiary bodies referred to in the preceding paragraph may adopt and amend their own rules of procedure, which shall be approved by the Committee on Commodity Problems and shall be consistent with the rules of the Committee.

Rule XXX

Committee on Fisheries

1. The Committee on Fisheries provided for in paragraph 6 of Article V of the Constitution shall be open to all Member Nations of the Organization. It shall be composed of those Member Nations which notify the Director-General in writing of their desire to become Members of the Committee and of their intention to participate in the work of the Committee.

2. The notification referred to in paragraph 1 may be made at any time and membership acquired on the basis thereof shall be for a biennium. The Director-General shall circulate, at the beginning of each session of the Committee, a document listing the Members of the Committee.

3. The Committee shall elect its own Chairman from among its Members.

4. The Committee shall normally hold two sessions during each biennium, to be convened by the Director-General in consultation with the Chairman of the Committee, taking into account any proposals made by the Committee. One of these sessions shall be convened sufficiently in advance of the session of the Council held approximately midway between the regular sessions of the Conference, in order that the report of the Committee may be circulated to the Members of the Council, in accordance with the provisions of Rule XXV.7 (*a*) of these Rules.

5. If required, the Committee may hold additional sessions on the call of its Chairman or the Director-General or on request submitted in writing to the Director-General by a majority of the Members of the Committee.

6. The Committee shall:

(*a*) review the programmes of work of the Organization in the field of fisheries and their implementation;

(*b*) conduct periodic general reviews of fishery problems of an international character and appraise such problems and their possible solutions with a view to concerted action by nations, by FAO and by other intergovernmental bodies;

(*c*) similarly review specific matters relating to fisheries referred to the Committee by the Council or the Director-General, or placed by the Committee on its agenda at the request of a Member Nation in accordance with the Rules of Procedure of the Committee, and make recommendations as may be appropriate;

(*d*) consider the desirability of preparing and submitting to Member Nations an international convention under Article XIV of the Constitution to ensure effective international cooperation and consultation in fisheries on a world scale;

(*e*) report to the Council or tender advice to the Director-General, as appropriate, on matters considered by the Committee.

7. Any recommendation adopted by the Committee which affects the programme or finances of the Organization shall be reported to the Council with the comments of the appropriate subsidiary committees of the Council. The reports of the Committee should, as in the case of certain other committees established under Article V of the Constitution, also be placed before the Conference.

8. The Director-General or his representative shall participate in all meetings of the Committee and may be accompanied by such officers of the staff of the Organization as he may designate.

9. The Committee may adopt and amend its own Rules of Procedure, which shall be consistent with the Constitution and the General Rules of the Organization.

10. The Committee may, when necessary, establish subcommittees, subsidiary working parties or study groups subject to the necessary funds being available in the relevant chapter of the approved budget of the Organization, and may include in the membership of such subcommittees, subsidiary working parties or study groups Member Nations that are not Members of the Committee and Associate Members. The Council may admit to membership

of subcommittees, subsidiary working parties and study groups established by the Committee States which, while not Member Nations or Associate Members of the Organization, are members of the United Nations, any of its specialized agencies or the International Atomic Energy Agency. Former Member Nations of the Organization that have withdrawn leaving arrears of contributions shall not be admitted to membership until such time as they have paid up all such arrears, or the Conference has approved an arrangement for the settlement thereof, or unless the Council in special circumstances decides otherwise with respect to such admission.

11. The subsidiary bodies referred to in the preceding paragraph may adopt or amend their own rules of procedure, which shall be approved by the Committee on Fisheries and shall be consistent with the rules of the Committee.

Rule XXXI

Committee on Forestry

1. The Committee on Forestry provided for in paragraph 6 of Article V of the Constitution shall be open to all Member Nations of the Organization. It shall be composed of those Member Nations which notify the Director-General in writing of their desire to become Members of the Committee and of their intention to participate in the work of the Committee.

2. The notification referred to in paragraph 1 may be made at any time and membership acquired on the basis thereof shall be for a biennium. The Director-General shall circulate, at the beginning of each session of the Committee, a document listing the Members of the Committee.

3. Sessions of the Committee shall normally be held once in each biennium, preferably early in non-Conference years. Sessions shall be convened by the Director-General in consultation with the Chairman of the Committee, taking into account any proposals made by the Committee.

4. If required, the Committee may hold additional sessions on the call of its Chairman or the Director-General, or on request submitted in writing to the Director-General by the majority of the Members of the Committee.

5. Members of the Committee should as far as possible be represented by their most senior officers responsible for forestry.

6. The Committee shall:

(*a*) conduct periodic reviews of forestry problems of an international character and appraise such problems with a view to concerted action which could be undertaken by Member Nations and the Organization in order to resolve such problems;

(*b*) review the programmes of work of the Organization in the field of forestry and their implementation;

(*c*) advise the Director-General on the future programmes of work of the Organization in the field of forestry and on their implementation;

(*d*) review specific matters relating to forestry referred to the Committee by the Council or the Director-General, or placed by the Committee on its agenda at the request of a Member Nation in accordance with the Rules of Procedure of the Committee, and make recommendations as may be appropriate;

(*e*) report to the Council and tender advice to the Director-General, as appropriate, on matters considered by the Committee.

7. Any recommendation adopted by the Committee which affects the programme or finances of the Organization shall be reported to the Council with the comments of the appropriate subsidiary committees of the Council. The reports of the Committee should, as in the case of certain other committees established under Article V of the Constitution, also be placed before the Conference.

8. The Director-General or his representative shall participate in all meetings of the Committee and may be accompanied by such officers of the staff of the Organization as he may designate.

9. The Committee shall elect its own Chairman from among its Members. It may adopt and amend its own Rules of Procedure, which shall be consistent with the Constitution and the General Rules of the Organization.

10. The Committee may, when necessary, establish subcommittees, subsidiary working parties or study groups, subject to the necessary funds being available in the relevant chapter of the approved budget of the Organization, and may include in the membership of such subcommittees, subsidiary working parties or study groups Member Nations that are not Members of the Committee and Associate Members. The Council may admit to membership of subcommittees, subsidiary working parties and study groups established by

the Committee States which, while not Member Nations or Associate Members of the Organization, are members of the United Nations, any of its specialized agencies or the International Atomic Energy Agency. Former Member Nations of the Organization that have withdrawn leaving arrears of contributions shall not be admitted to membership of subcommittees, subsidiary working parties and study groups until such time as they have paid up all such arrears, or the Conference has approved an arrangement for the settlement thereof, or unless the Council in special circumstances decides otherwise with respect to such admission.

11. The subsidiary bodies referred to in the preceding paragraph may adopt or amend their own rules of procedure, which shall be approved by the Committee on Forestry and shall be consistent with the rules of the Committee.

Rule XXXII

Committee on Agriculture

1. The Committee on Agriculture provided for in paragraph 6 of Article V of the Constitution shall be open to all Member Nations of the Organization. It shall be composed of those Member Nations which notify the Director-General in writing of their desire to become Members of the Committee and of their intention to participate in the work of the Committee.

2. The notification referred to in paragraph 1 may be made at any time and membership acquired on the basis thereof shall be for a biennium. The Director-General shall circulate, at the beginning of each session of the Committee, a document listing the Members of the Committee.

3. Sessions of the Committee shall normally be held once in each biennium, preferably early in Conference years. Sessions shall be convened by the Director-General in consultation with the Chairman of the Committee, taking into account any proposals made by the Committee.

4. If required, the Committee may hold additional sessions on the call of the Director-General in consultation with its Chairman, or on request submitted in writing to the Director-General by the majority of the Members of the Committee.

5. Members of the Committee should, as far as possible, be represented by delegations consisting of senior officers highly qualified to contribute actively to a multidisciplinary consideration of the subjects on the agenda of the Committee.

6. The Committee shall:

(*a*) conduct periodic reviews and appraisals, on a highly selective basis, of agricultural and nutrition problems, with a view to concerted action by Member Nations and the Organization;

(*b*) advise the Council on the overall medium- and longer-term programme of work of the Organization relating to agriculture, food and nutrition, with emphasis on the integration of all social, technical, economic, institutional and structural aspects related to agricultural and rural development in general;

(*c*) review, with similar emphasis, the biennial programmes of work of the Organization and their implementation in areas falling within the competence of the Committee;

(*d*) review specific matters relating to agriculture, food and nutrition referred to the Committee by the Conference, the Council or the Director-General, or placed by the Committee on its agenda at the request of a Member Nation in accordance with the Rules of Procedure of the Committee, and make recommendations as may be appropriate;

(*e*) report to the Council and tender advice to the Director-General, as appropriate, on any other matter considered by the Committee.

7. For the purpose of the present Rule, the term "agriculture" does not include fishery and forestry matters which are within the terms of reference of the Committee on Fisheries and the Committee on Forestry respectively.

8. The Committee shall establish appropriate procedures for determining its agenda in respect of each session, bearing in mind the desirability of ensuring an interdisciplinary consideration of all relevant aspects of a limited number of major issues, and taking into account the basic responsibility of the Committee on Commodity Problems for reviewing commodity and related trade problems of an international character.

9. Any recommendation adopted by the Committee affecting the programme or finances of the Organization or concerning legal or constitutional

matters shall be reported to the Council with the comments of the appropriate subsidiary committees of the Council. The reports of the Committee shall also be placed before the Conference.

10. The Director-General or his representative shall participate in all meetings of the Committee and may be accompanied by such officers of the staff of the Organization as he may designate.

11. The Committee shall elect from among its Members its Chairman and the other officers. It may adopt and amend its Rules of Procedure, which shall be consistent with the Constitution and the General Rules of the Organization.

12. The Committee may, on an exceptional basis, establish subsidiary or ad hoc bodies where it considers that such action is conducive to facilitating its own work and will not adversely affect the multidisciplinary consideration of questions submitted to the Committee for examination. Before taking a decision on the establishment of any subsidiary or ad hoc body, the Committee shall examine the administrative and financial implications of such decision, in the light of a report to be submitted by the Director-General. The Committee shall define the terms of reference, composition and, as far as possible, the duration of the mandate of each subsidiary or ad hoc body.

13. (*a*) The Committee may include in the membership of such subsidiary or ad hoc bodies Member Nations that are not Members of the Committee and Associate Members.

(*b*) The Council may admit to membership of subsidiary or ad hoc bodies established by the Committee States which, while not Member Nations or Associate Members of the Organization, are members of the United Nations, any of its specialized agencies or the International Atomic Energy Agency.

(*c*) Former Member Nations of the Organization that have withdrawn leaving arrears of contributions shall not be admitted to membership of subsidiary or ad hoc bodies of the Committee until such time as they have paid up all such arrears, or the Conference has approved an arrangement for the settlement thereof, or unless the Council in special circumstances decides otherwise with respect to such admission.

14. The subsidiary or ad hoc bodies referred to in paragraph 12 may adopt or amend their rules of procedure, which shall be approved by the Committee and shall be consistent with its Rules of Procedure.

Rule XXXIII

Committee on World Food Security

1. The Committee on World Food Security provided for in paragraph 6 of Article V of the Constitution shall be open to all Member Nations of the Organization and all Member States of the United Nations. It shall be composed of those States which notify the Director-General in writing of their desire to become Members of the Committee and of their intention to participate in the work of the Committee.

2. The notifications referred to in paragraph 1 may be made at any time, and membership acquired on the basis thereof shall be for a biennium. The Director-General shall circulate, at the beginning of each session of the Committee, a document listing the Members of the Committee.

3. The Committee shall normally hold two sessions during each biennium. Sessions shall be convened by the Director-General, in consultation with the Chairman of the Committee, taking into account any proposals made by the Committee.

4. If required, the Committee may hold additional sessions on the call of the Director-General in consultation with its Chairman, or on request submitted in writing to the Director-General by the majority of Members of the Committee.

5. The Committee shall contribute to promoting the objective of world food security with the aim of ensuring that all people, at all times, have physical and economic access to sufficient, safe and nutritious food to meet their dietary needs and food preferences for an active and healthy life.

6. The Committee shall serve as a forum in the United Nations system for review and follow-up of policies concerning world food security, including food production, sustainable use of the natural resource base for food security, nutrition, physical and economic access to food and other food security related aspects of poverty eradication, the implications of food trade for world food security and other related matters and shall in particular:

(*a*) examine major problems and issues affecting the world food situation and the steps being proposed or taken to resolve them by Governments and relevant international organizations, bearing in mind the need for the adoption of an integrated approach towards their solution;

(*b*) examine the implications for world food security of other relevant factors, including the situation relating to the supply and demand of basic foodstuffs and food aid requirements and trends, the state of stocks in exporting and importing countries and issues relating to physical and economic access to food and other food security related aspects of poverty eradication; and

(*c*) recommend such action as may be appropriate to promote the goal of world food security.

7. The Committee shall serve as the forum in the United Nations system for the monitoring of the implementation of the Plan of Action adopted by the World Food Summit in accordance with the relevant commitment of the Summit.[1]

---

[1] The relevant provisions of the World Food Summit Plan of Action are set out in Commitment 7, Objective 7.3, which reads as follows:

"To monitor actively the implementation of the World Food Summit Plan of Action.

To this end, Government, in partnership with all actors of civil society, in coordination with relevant international institutions and, in conformity with ECOSOC Resolution 1996/36 on the follow-up to the major international UN conferences and summits as appropriate, will:

(*a*) Establish through the CFS a timetable, procedures and standardized reporting formats, which do not duplicate similar reports to the UN, FAO and other agencies, on the national, subregional and regional implementation of the World Food Summit Plan of Action;

(*b*) Set out in the CFS a process for developing targets and verifiable indicators of national and global food security where they do not exist;

(*c*) Report to the CFS on national, subregional and regional implementation of the World Food Summit Plan of Action, drawing on a food insecurity and vulnerability information and mapping system, once established, as an analytical aid;

(*d*) Invite the Secretary-General of the UN to request the ACC to report to ECOSOC in accordance with established procedures progress on the follow-up by UN agencies to the World Food Summit;

(*e*) Monitor through the CFS the national, subregional, regional and international implementation of the World Food Summit Plan of Action, using reports from national governments, reports on UN agency follow-up and interagency coordination, and information from other relevant international institutions;

(*f*) Provide regular reports on implementation of the World Food Summit Plan of Action through the CFS via the FAO Council to the ECOSOC;

(*g*) Encourage the effective participation of relevant actors of civil society in the CFS monitoring process, recognizing their critical role in enhancing food security;

(*h*) By 2006, undertake in the CFS and within available resources a major broad-based progress assessment of the implementation of the World Food Summit Plan of Action and a mid-term review of achieving the target of reducing the number of undernourished people to half their present level no later than 2015. This progress assessment and review should be in the context of a special forum of a regular session of the CFS and involve active participation from governments, relevant international organizations and actors of civil society."

8. The Committee shall report to the Council of the Organization and tender advice to the Director-General, and relevant international organizations as appropriate, on any matter considered by the Committee, it being understood that copies of its reports, including any conclusions, will be transmitted without delay to interested governments and international organizations.

9. The Committee shall provide regular reports to the Economic and Social Council of the United Nations (ECOSOC), through the Council of the Organization.

10. Any recommendation adopted by the Committee affecting the programme or finance of the Organization or concerning legal or constitutional matters shall be reported to the Council with the comments of the appropriate subsidiary committees of the Council. The reports of the Committee, or relevant extracts therefrom, shall also be placed before the Conference.

11. The Committee shall draw on the advice, as necessary, of the Committee on Commodity Problems and its subsidiary bodies, the Committee on Agriculture and other technical committees of the Council as appropriate, and the Executive Board of the World Food Programme. In particular, it shall take full account of the responsibilities and activities of these and other intergovernmental bodies responsible for aspects of food security, in order to avoid overlapping and unnecessary duplication of work.

12. The Committee shall invite relevant international organizations to participate in the work of the Committee and the preparation of meeting documents on matters within their respective mandates in collaboration with the secretariat of the Committee.

13. In order to ensure the effective discharge of its functions, the Committee may request the Members to furnish all information required for its work, it being understood that where so requested by the governments concerned, the information supplied shall be kept on a restricted basis.

14. The Director-General or his representative shall participate in all meetings of the Committee and may be accompanied by such officers of the staff of the Organization as he may designate.

15. The Committee shall elect, from among its Members, its Chairman and the other officers. It may adopt and amend its rules of procedure, which shall be consistent with the Constitution and the General Rules of the Organization.

16. The Committee may decide to establish subsidiary or ad hoc bodies where it considers that such action would expedite its own work, without duplicating the work of existing bodies. A decision to this effect may be taken only after the Committee has examined a report by the Director-General on the administrative and financial implications.

17. When establishing subsidiary or ad hoc bodies, the Committee shall define their terms of reference, composition, and, as far as possible, the duration of their mandate. Subsidiary bodies may adopt their own rules of procedure, which shall be consistent with those of the Committee.

Rule XXXIV

Committee on Constitutional and Legal Matters

1. The Committee on Constitutional and Legal Matters provided for in paragraph 6 of Article V of the Constitution shall be composed of not more than seven Member Nations elected by the Council for a period of two years at the session of the Council immediately following the regular session of the Conference.

2. Nomination of any candidate for election to the Committee shall be submitted in writing by one or more Member Nations to the Secretary-General of the Conference and Council by a deadline to be determined by the Chairman of the Council in time to be circulated on the morning of the day set for the election. A Member Nation may nominate itself. Member Nations nominated shall signify their willingness to serve on the Committee if elected. The provisions on voting arrangements of Rule XII of these Rules shall apply *mutatis mutandis* to the election of Members of the Committee.

3. The Committee shall hold sessions to consider specific items referred to it by the Council or the Director-General which may arise out of:

(*a*) the application or interpretation of the Constitution, these Rules and the Financial Regulations or amendments thereto;

(*b*) the formulation, adoption, entry into force and interpretation of multilateral conventions and agreements concluded under Article XIV of the Constitution;

(*c*) the formulation, adoption, entry into force and interpretation of agreements to which the Organization is a party under Articles XIII and XV of the Constitution;

(*d*) any other problems relating to conventions and agreements concluded under the aegis of the Organization or to which the Organization is a party;

(*e*) the establishment of commissions and committees under Article VI of the Constitution, including their membership, terms of reference, reporting procedures and rules of procedure;

(*f*) matters relating to membership in the Organization and its relations with nations;

(*g*) the desirability of requesting advisory opinions from the International Court of Justice in accordance with paragraph 2 of Article XVII of the Constitution, or with the Statute of the Administrative Tribunal of the International Labour Organisation;

(*h*) the policy regarding privileges and immunities to be sought from host governments for the Organization's headquarters, regional offices, country representations, conferences and meetings;

(*i*) problems encountered ensuring the immunity of the Organization, its staff and its assets;

(*j*) problems relating to elections and procedure for nominations;

(*k*) standards for credentials and full powers;

(*l*) reports on the status of conventions and agreements provided for in Rule XXI, paragraph 5 of these Rules;

(*m*) policy aspects of relations with international governmental or non-governmental organizations, national institutions or private persons.

4. The Committee may also consider the legal and constitutional aspects of any other matters submitted to it by the Council or the Director-General.

5. In considering items referred to it under paragraphs 3 and 4, the Committee may make recommendations and give advisory opinion, as appropriate.

6. The Committee shall elect a Chairman and a Vice-Chairman from among its Members.

7. The meetings of the Committee shall be held in private, unless otherwise determined by the Committee.

8. The Committee may adopt and amend its own Rules of Procedure, which shall be consistent with the Constitution and these Rules.

Rule XXXV

Commissions, committees and working parties

1. Commissions, committees and working parties set up in pursuance of Article VI of the Constitution may establish subcommissions, subcommittees or subsidiary working parties either to perform a substantive part of their functions or to carry out a specific task. Associate Members may participate in the deliberations of such subcommissions, subcommittees or subsidiary working parties but shall not hold office or have the right to vote.

2. The first paragraph of this Rule shall be interpreted in conformity with the provisions of Rule XXIV, paragraph 1 (*d*) (*v*) of these Rules.

3. A panel of experts, as referred to in Article VI, paragraph 4 of the Constitution, is a list of experts selected in their individual capacity on the basis of their expert knowledge to give advice on specific subjects by correspondence, or by participation in conferences or consultations when it is so decided by the Director-General.

4. The terms of office of members of committees of experts or working parties of experts appointed in their personal capacity in conformity with paragraph 2 of Article VI of the Constitution shall not exceed four years but shall be renewable. The terms of office of members of panels of experts shall likewise be for a maximum of four years but shall be renewable. Appointments to fill vacancies in committees of experts, working parties of experts and panels of experts shall be effected in the same manner as the original appointments. When a vacancy occurs due to resignation, death, disability or any other reason, the terms of office of the new appointee shall be for the remainder of the term of office of the member who is being replaced.

5. Unless other specific arrangements are made, the expenses incurred by individuals invited in a personal capacity to attend sessions of committees of experts or working parties of experts, or conferences or consultations of experts shall be defrayed by the Organization in accordance with its travel regulations.

C. THE DIRECTOR-GENERAL AND STAFF

Rule XXXVI

Appointment of the Director-General

1. In pursuance of paragraph 1 of Article VII of the Constitution, the Director-General of the Organization shall be appointed under the following conditions:

(*a*) When the term of office of the Director-General is due to expire, the appointment of a new Director-General shall be placed on the agenda of the regular session of the Conference immediately preceding the expiry of the term of office; whenever, for other reasons, the office of the Director-General is vacant, or notice is received of a pending vacancy, the appointment of a new Director-General shall be placed on the agenda of the next session of the Conference which opens not less than 90 days from the occurrence or notice of the pending vacancy. Nominations validly made in accordance with Rule XII.5 of these Rules shall be communicated to the Secretary-General of the Conference and Council by the date set by the Council. The Secretary-General shall circulate these nominations to all Member Nations and Associate Members by the date likewise set by the Council, it being understood that in the case of an election taking place at a regular session of the Conference, such date set by the Council shall be not later than 30 days before the session of the Council provided for in Rule XXV.2 (*c*) of these Rules. As soon as possible after the opening of the Conference session, the General Committee shall determine and announce the date of the election, it being understood that the appointment of the Director-General at a regular session shall begin and be effected within three working days following the opening date of such session.

(*b*) The Director-General shall be elected by a majority of votes cast. Until a candidate obtains the required majority, the following procedure shall apply:

- (*i*) two ballots shall be held among all candidates;
- (*ii*) the candidate having received the smallest number of votes in the second ballot shall be eliminated;

(*iii*) thereafter, successive ballots shall be held, and the candidate having received the smallest number of votes in any one of these ballots shall be eliminated, until only three candidates remain;

(*iv*) two ballots shall be held among the three remaining candidates;

(*v*) the candidate having received the smallest number of votes during the second ballot referred to in subparagraph (*iv*) above shall be eliminated;

(*vi*) a subsequent ballot, or successive ballots if necessary, shall be held among the two remaining candidates until one candidate obtains the required majority;

(*vii*) in the event of a tie between two or more candidates having received the smallest number of votes in one of the ballots referred to in subparagraphs (*ii*) or (*iii*) above, a separate ballot or, if necessary, separate ballots shall be held among such candidates, and the candidate having received the smallest number of votes in such ballot or ballots shall be eliminated;

(*viii*) in the event of a tie between two candidates having received the smallest number of votes in the second of the two ballots referred to in subparagraph (*iv*) above, or if all three candidates have received the same number of votes in that ballot, successive ballots shall be held among all three candidates until one candidate has received the smallest number of votes, after which the procedure provided in subparagraph (*vi*) above shall apply.

(*c*) Subject to the provisions of Article VII, paragraphs 1 to 3 of the Constitution, the terms and conditions of appointment of the Director-General, including the salary and other emoluments attached to the office, shall be determined by the Conference, having regard to any recommendations submitted by the General Committee, and shall be embodied in a contract signed by him and by the Chairman of the Conference on behalf of the Organization.

2. The Deputy Director-General shall act as Director-General in any case where the Director-General is unable to act or in the case of a vacancy in the office of the Director-General.

Rule XXXVII

Functions of the Director-General

1. The Director-General shall have full powers and authority to direct the work of the Organization, subject to the general supervision of the Conference and of the Council and in accordance with these Rules and the Financial Regulations. The Director-General is the executive officer of the Organization, and as such shall service the Conference and Council, carry out their decisions, and act on behalf of the Organization in all its transactions.

2. In particular, the Director-General shall, in accordance with these Rules and the Financial Regulations, and provided that he reports to the Council or Conference as appropriate on all matters involving policy issues:

(*a*) be responsible for the internal administration of the Organization and for the appointment and discipline of the staff;

(*b*) convene the sessions of the Conference and Council;

(*c*) publish annually and communicate to Member Nations and Associate Members a detailed world survey of the state of food and agriculture;

(*d*) present a report on the work of the Organization at each regular session of the Conference;

(*e*) carry out the duties with regard to conventions and agreements laid down in these Rules;

(*f*) receive applications for admission to the Organization;

(*g*) prepare:

  (*i*) in the light of guidance given by the Conference and Council at previous sessions and by regional and technical conferences, commissions or committees, a summary Programme of Work and Budget for consideration by the Programme and Finance Committees, other appropriate organs of the Organization, and the Council; and

  (*ii*) in the light of the observations by the aforementioned Committees and organs and by the Council, a draft Programme of Work and Budget for submission to the Conference;

(*h*) prepare and submit the accounts of the Organization;

(*i*) prepare a report on the state of food and agriculture for submission to the regular session of the Conference as provided in Rule II.2 (*c*) (*i*);

(*j*) request and receive payments of contributions of Member Nations and Associate Members and report thereon;

(*k*) conduct the relations of the Organization with other international organizations, and provide liaison with intergovernmental commodity bodies and with United Nations agencies;

(*l*) perform such other duties as are provided for in these Rules and the Financial Regulations, or any other rules and regulations from time to time in force.

3. Pursuant to Article VI of the Constitution, the Director-General may:

(*a*) establish:

(*i*) panels of experts;

(*ii*) committees or working parties when he is satisfied that urgent action is required;

(*b*) convene:

(*i*) commissions, committees, working parties or meetings of members of panels;

(*ii*) general, regional, technical or other conferences, or working parties or consultations of Member Nations and Associate Members, on the authority of the Conference or Council, or on his own initiative, when he is satisfied that urgent action is required.

4. When determining the site of any meeting to be convened by the Organization, the Director-General should be satisfied that the host government is willing to grant to all delegates, representatives, experts, observers and members of the Secretariat of the Organization attending such a meeting the immunities that are necessary for the independent exercise of their functions in connection with the meeting.

Rule XXXVIII

Consultation by the Director-General with governments under Article XIII, paragraph 4 of the Constitution

1. In order to secure proper consultation with governments under Article XIII, paragraph 4 of the Constitution, the procedure, in general, shall be that the Director-General shall not establish formal or official relations with

nationals or national institutions without consulting in advance the Member Nation or Associate Member concerned.

2. When a Member Nation or Associate Member has established a National FAO Committee, the Committee may, with the specific concurrence of the interested government, be utilized as a suitable instrument for coordinating the participation of the said Member Nation or Associate Member in the activities of the Organization, under such conditions as the government may have determined.

Rule XXXIX

Provisions relating to staff

1. The staff of the Organization shall be appointed by the Director-General, having regard to paragraph 3 of Article VIII of the Constitution. Selection and remuneration shall be made without regard to race, nationality, creed or sex. The terms and conditions of appointment shall be fixed in contracts concluded between the Director-General and each member of the staff. Appointment to the post of Deputy Director-General shall be made by the Director-General, subject to confirmation by the Council.

2. The Director-General shall submit proposals to the Finance Committee on the scale of salaries and conditions of recruitment and service of the staff and shall report to the Finance Committee and the Council any decisions or recommendations of the International Civil Service Commission relating to such matters. He shall submit proposals to the Finance Committee on the general structure of the administrative and technical services of the Organization. He shall, insofar as may be feasible, arrange for public announcements of staff vacancies and shall fill vacancies in accordance with such competitive methods of selection as he may consider most suitable for various types of appointment.

3. The Director-General, with the approval of the Council, shall promulgate such general staff regulations as may be necessary, including the requirement of a declaration of loyalty to the Organization. The Director-General shall have authority to promulgate Staff Regulations to give effect to decisions of the International Civil Service Commission, as well as to give effect to recommendations of the International Civil Service Commission which have been approved by the General Assembly of the United Nations with regard to the

salaries and allowances of the staff in the professional and higher categories. He shall report the promulgation of such Staff Regulations to the Finance Committee and the Council.

4. Except as provided in paragraph 1 of this Rule, the Director-General shall act in his unfettered judgement in appointing, assigning and promoting staff personnel, and shall not be bound to accept advice or request from any other source.

5. The Director-General shall have disciplinary control over the members of the staff, including the power of dismissal, except that in the case of the Deputy Director-General the approval of the Council must be obtained for dismissal.

6. The Director-General shall arrange for consultation between the Organization and the United Nations with regard to the establishment of common machinery for the settlement of matters of dispute between the employees and the Organization which have not been settled by internal conciliation.

D. MEMBER ORGANIZATIONS

Rule XL

General

The provisions of the General Rules of the Organization applicable to Member Nations shall apply *mutatis mutandis* to Member Organizations, except as may be otherwise provided in the Constitution or in these General Rules.

Rule XLI

Competence

1. Any Member Nation of the Organization may request a Member Organization or its Member States to provide information as to which, as between the Member Organization and its Member States, has competence in respect of any specific question. The Member Organization or the Member States concerned shall provide this information on such request.

2. Before any meeting of the Organization the Member Organization or its Member States shall indicate which, as between the Member Organization and its Member States, has competence in respect of any specific question to be considered in the meeting and which, as between the Member Organization and its Member States, shall exercise the right to vote in respect of each particular agenda item.

3. In cases where an agenda item covers both matters in respect of which competence has been transferred to the Member Organization and matters which lie within the competence of its Member States, both the Member Organization and its Member States may participate in the discussions. In such cases the meeting, in arriving at its decisions, shall take into account only the intervention of the party which has the right to vote.

Rule XLII

Arrangements for the Conference

1. The credentials of delegates, alternates, associates and advisers of a Member Organization to sessions of the Conference shall be issued by, or on behalf of, the head of the executive body of the Member Organization concerned.

2. Member Organizations shall not participate in the Credentials Committee or the General Committee or any other body of the Conference dealing with the internal working of the Conference as the Conference may decide.

3. Member Organizations shall not hold office in the Conference or any subsidiary body of the Conference.

Rule XLIII

Arrangements for the Council

Member Organizations shall not hold office in the Council or any subsidiary body of the Council.

Rule XLIV

Quorum and voting arrangements at meetings of the Conference and Council

1. For the purpose of determining a quorum, as specified in paragraph 2 (*b*) of Rule XII, the delegation of a Member Organization shall be counted to the extent that it is entitled to vote in the meeting in respect of which the quorum is sought.

2. Member Organizations shall not participate in voting for elective places as defined in paragraph 9 (*a*) of Rule XII.

Rule XLV

Arrangements regarding committees of restricted membership

Member Organizations shall not participate in the Programme Committee, the Finance Committee and the Committee on Constitutional and Legal Matters.

E. MISCELLANEOUS PROVISIONS

Rule XLVI

Seat of the Organization

The seat of the Organization shall be in Rome, Italy.

Rule XLVII

Languages

Arabic, Chinese, English, French and Spanish are the languages of the Organization.

Rule XLVIII

Suspension and amendment of Rules

1. Subject to the provisions of the Constitution, any of the foregoing Rules may be suspended by a two-thirds majority of the votes cast at any plenary meeting of the Conference, provided that notice of the intention to propose the suspension has been communicated to the delegates not less than 24 hours before the meeting at which the proposal is to be made.

2. Amendments of, or additions to, these Rules may be adopted by a two-thirds majority of the votes cast at any plenary meeting of the Conference, provided that the intention to propose the amendment or addition has been communicated to the delegates not less than 24 hours before the meeting at which the proposal is to be considered, and provided further that the Conference has received and considered a report on the proposal by an appropriate committee.

3. The Council may propose amendments and additions to these Rules and any such proposals may be considered at the next session of the Conference.

Regulation I

Applicability

1.1 These regulations shall govern the financial administration of the Food and Agriculture Organization of the United Nations.

Regulation II

The financial period

2.1 The financial period shall be two calendar years, in accordance with Article XVIII, paragraph 4 of the Constitution.

Regulation III

The budget

3.1 The budget estimates shall be prepared by the Director-General.

3.2 The estimates shall cover income and expenditures for the financial period to which they relate, and shall be presented in United States dollars.

3.3 The budget estimates shall be presented on a programme-budget basis and divided into chapters and programme objectives, and where necessary into programmes and subprogrammes. The budget estimates shall include the programme of work for the financial period, such information, annexes or explanatory statements as may be requested on behalf of the Conference or the Council, and such further annexes or statements as the Director-General may deem appropriate.

3.4 The Director-General shall submit to the regular session of the Conference detailed budget estimates for the ensuing financial period. The estimates shall be dispatched to all Member Nations and Associate Members not less than 60 days before the date fixed for the opening of the session.

3.5 The Director-General shall arrange for the summary budget to be considered by the Council not less than 90 days before the date fixed for the opening of the regular session of the Conference.

3.6 The Council shall prepare a report to the Conference on the estimates submitted by the Director-General. This report shall be transmitted to all Member Nations and Associate Members at the same time as the estimates.

3.7 The budget for the ensuing financial period shall be adopted by the Conference at its regular session, after due consideration of the estimates.

3.8 Supplementary estimates to cover emergency expenditure in accordance with Regulation 6.3 may be submitted by the Director-General when and as he may deem necessary.

3.9 The Director-General shall prepare supplementary estimates in a form consistent with the estimates for the financial period and shall submit such estimates to the Conference and to the Council. The Council shall review such estimates and report thereon to the Conference.

Regulation IV

Appropriations

4.1 (*a*) The appropriations voted by the Conference for the ensuing financial period shall constitute an authorization to the Director-General to incur obligations and make payments for the purpose for which the appropriations were voted, and up to the amounts so voted.

(*b*) The Director-General may also incur obligations against future periods before appropriations are voted when such obligations are necessary for the continued effective functioning of the Organization, provided such obligations are restricted to administrative requirements of a continuing nature not exceeding the scale of such requirements as authorized in the budget of the current financial period.

4.2 Except as provided for in Financial Regulation 4.3 relating to the

Technical Cooperation Programme, appropriations shall be available for obligations during the financial period to which they relate and unobligated appropriations at the close of the financial period shall be cancelled.

4.3 Appropriations voted by the Conference for the Technical Cooperation Programme, together with any funds transferred to the Technical Cooperation Programme under Financial Regulation 4.5 (*b*), shall remain available for obligations during the financial period following that during which the funds were voted or transferred. Appropriations unutilized at the close of the financial period following that during which the funds were voted or transferred shall be cancelled.

4.4 Such portion of appropriations as may be required to meet the outstanding legal obligations as at the last day of the financial period shall remain available for 12 months, except that in the case of outstanding legal obligations in respect of fellowships the portion of the appropriation required shall remain available until the fellowship is completed or otherwise terminated. At the end of 12 months, or in the case of fellowships at the termination of the fellowship, any remaining balances shall be credited to Miscellaneous Income of the current financial period. Any obligations (except for fellowships) remaining a valid claim at that time shall be charged against the appropriations of the current financial period.

4.5 (*a*) Transfers within the same chapter of the budget may be effected by the Director-General. He shall report such transfers to the Finance Committee in instances where funds are moved from one Division (or equivalent unit) to another and where, in addition, the amount involved in each such transfer exceeds a specific sum established in accordance with the provisions of Financial Regulation 10.1 (*a*) and of the General Rules of the Organization.

(*b*) (*i*) Transfers from one chapter of the budget to another relating to expenditures which would not involve additional financial obligations for Member Nations and Associate Members, either current or future, may be effected by the Director-General after having obtained the approval of the Finance Committee, or by the Council between sessions of the Finance Committee.

(*ii*) Transfers from one chapter of the budget to another, other than those for which the Finance Committee has authority, may be effected by the Director-General after having obtained the approval of the Council.

(*c*) (*i*) The expenditure of any sum (or part thereof) which may have been voted in the budget to cover unforeseen contingencies may be effected by the Director-General.

(*ii*) Any savings which accrue during the operations of a financial period may be transferred by the Director-General to the Contingencies chapter. The transfer of such savings from Contingencies shall be subject to the approval of the Finance Committee or of the Council, as set out in Regulation 4.5 (*b*).

4.6 (*a*) The Director-General shall so apportion and manage appropriations made for the financial period as to ensure that adequate funds will be available to meet expenditures during the entire financial period, and that the obligations and expenditures follow, in general, the financial plans contemplated by the Programme of Work and Budget approved by the Conference. There shall be no concentration of obligations or expenditure in any one calendar year, except as approved by the Conference, and under no circumstance shall any savings accruing during the financial period be used for any projects or activities which may involve additional obligations for Member Nations and Associate Members in future financial periods for the continuation of such projects or activities.

(*b*) The Finance Committee shall review annually the Director-General's fund allotment and apportionment controls to determine that they meet adequately the objectives of this regulation.

Regulation V

Provision of funds

5.1 The appropriations for a financial period, subject to related adjustments effected in accordance with Regulation 5.2, shall be financed by annual contributions from Member Nations and Associate Members. Contributions from Member Nations shall be assessed in accordance with the scale of contributions determined by the Conference, which scale shall not include contributions from Associate Members. Contributions from Associate Members shall as far as feasible be calculated on the same basis as contributions from Member Nations, the amount thus obtained being reduced by four tenths to take account of the difference of status between Member Nations and Associate Members, and shall be credited to Miscellaneous Income. Pending receipt of contributions, appropriations may be financed from the Working Capital Fund.

5.2 In the assessment of the contributions of Member Nations and Associate Members for each financial period, adjustments shall be made in respect of:

(*a*) estimated Miscellaneous Income of the financial period in respect of which the assessment of contributions is being made;

(*b*) credits accruing to Member Nations as a result of the application of Financial Regulation 6.1 (*b*);

(*c*) supplementary appropriations for which contributions have not previously been assessed on the Member Nations and Associate Members.

5.3 For determining the annual contribution of each Member Nation and Associate Member, the assessment of each such Member Nation and Associate Member for the financial period shall be divided into two equal instalments, one of which shall be payable in the first calendar year and the other in the second calendar year of the financial period.

5.4 At the beginning of each calendar year the Director-General shall:

(*a*) inform Member Nations and Associate Members of their obligations in respect of annual contributions to the budget;

(*b*) inform Member Nations of their obligations in respect of advances to the Working Capital Fund;

(*c*) request Member Nations and Associate Members, as the case may be, to remit all contributions and advances due.

5.5 Contributions and advances shall be due and payable in full within 30 days of the receipt of the communication of the Director-General referred to in Regulation 5.4 above, or as of the first day of the calendar year to which they relate, whichever is the later. As of 1 January of the following calendar year, the unpaid balance of such contributions and advances shall be considered to be one year in arrears.

5.6 Annual contributions to the budget shall be assessed in United States dollars. To the extent that the Conference, after ascertaining in what currencies Member Nations and Associate Members propose to make their contributions in the ensuing financial period, finds that anticipated United States dollar income will be inadequate to meet estimated United States dollar expenditures of the Organization as determined by the Conference, the Conference will determine the proportionate share of contribution that all Member Nations and Associate Members who do not pay their contributions in full in

United States dollars shall pay in that currency. Each Member Nation and Associate Member shall pay the remainder of its contribution in lire, or in its own currency which, for the purposes of its contributions to the Organization, must be freely convertible into lire, the convertibility being the responsibility of the contributing government. The applicable rate shall be the official rate of the lire to the dollar on the first business day in January of the calendar year in which the contribution is due, or the rate in effect on the day the payment is made, whichever is the higher.

5.7 Obligations of Member Nations and Associate Members, including arrears of contribution, shall remain payable in the currency of contribution of the year in which they were due.

5.8 Any nation admitted to membership or any territory or group of territories admitted to associate membership shall pay a contribution to the budget for the financial period in which the membership or associate membership becomes effective. Such contributions shall be an amount determined by the Conference and shall begin with the quarter in which the application was approved. All new Member Nations shall be required to make advances to the Working Capital Fund in accordance with Regulation 6.2 (*b*) (*ii*).

5.9 Non-member nations of the Organization that are members of intergovernmental commodity groups; subcommittees, subsidiary working parties and study groups established by the Committee on Fisheries; or of bodies established by conventions or agreements concluded under Article XIV of the Constitution shall contribute towards the expenses incurred by the Organization with respect to the activities of those groups or bodies in an amount determined by the Director-General except as otherwise decided by the Conference or the Council.

5.10 The Council, at any of its sessions, may advise the Director-General as to any steps that ought to be taken in order to expedite the payment of contributions. The Council may submit to the Conference such recommendations in this regard as it may consider appropriate.

Regulation VI

Funds

6.1 (*a*) There shall be established a General Fund to which shall be credited receipts from contributions of Member Nations, whether current or arrears, Miscellaneous Income and advances made from the Working Capital Fund; and from which shall be made all general expenditures and reimbursements to the Working Capital Fund under Financial Regulation 6.5 (*a*).

(*b*) Any cash surplus in the General Fund at the close of any financial period shall be allocated among Member Nations in accordance with the Scale of Contributions applicable to that period and, as of 1 January following the year in which the audit of the final accounts of the financial period is completed, shall be released and applied to liquidate, in whole or in part, first, any advance due to the Working Capital Fund; second, any arrears of contributions; and third, contributions for the calendar year following the year in which the audit is completed.

6.2 (*a*) There shall be maintained a Working Capital Fund in United States dollars in such amount as the Conference shall determine from time to time for:

(*i*) advancing moneys to the General Fund to finance budgetary expenditures pending receipt of contributions to the budget;

(*ii*) advancing moneys to the General Fund to finance emergency expenditures not provided for in the current budget;

(*iii*) making reimbursable loans for such purposes as the Council may authorize in specific cases. Advances made by the Working Capital Fund for these purposes shall be considered as forming part of the Fund.

(*b*) The amount of the Working Capital Fund thus determined shall be contributed by Member Nations in United States dollars in accordance with the following provisions:

(*i*) Member Nations shall be assessed as of 1 January 1956 in accordance with the Scale of Contributions for 1956. Any amounts standing to their credit in the Fund on 31 December 1955 shall be applied against this assessment.

(*ii*) A new Member Nation shall be assessed in an amount determined by the Conference. Unless the Conference decides otherwise, the amount of the new Member Nation's assessment shall be considered as an increase to the level of the Working Capital Fund.

(*iii*) The assessment of Member Nations in the Working Capital Fund, effected under subparagraph (*i*) above, shall not be changed by modifications in the Scale of Contributions or in the membership of the Organization, unless the Conference decides otherwise.

(*iv*) If the Conference decides to change the level of the Working Capital Fund, there shall be a reassessment.

(*v*) Any reassessment shall be applied as from the first day of the financial period following the Conference determination and calculated in accordance with the Scale of Contributions of the financial period.

(*vi*) On reassessment, any excess of credits due to Member Nations shall be released immediately from the Working Capital Fund and applied (after any General Fund surplus has been released and applied in accordance with the provisions of Financial Regulation 6.1 [*b*]) first, to contributions in arrears; second, to current contributions; and third, refunded or applied against future contributions at the option of Member Nations.

6.3 Withdrawals from the Working Capital Fund for financing emergency expenditures shall be approved in advance by the Council.

6.4 Moneys provided by each Member Nation under Regulation 6.2 (*b*) shall be carried to the credit of that Member Nation in the Working Capital Fund.

6.5 (*a*) Advances made from the Working Capital Fund to finance budgetary expenditure under Financial Regulation 6.2 (*a*) (*i*) shall be reimbursed from the General Fund as soon as feasible, but in any case within the next financial period, by programme adjustments if necessary.

(*b*) Advances made from the Working Capital Fund to finance emergency expenditure under Financial Regulation 6.2 (*a*) (*ii*) shall be reimbursed by such method as the Conference determines.

6.6 (*a*) Income derived from the investment of the Working Capital Fund shall be credited to the Miscellaneous Income of the Organization, and shall accrue to the General Fund.

(*b*) If a Nation withdraws its membership in the Organization, any credit it may have in the Working Capital Fund shall be used towards liquidation of any financial obligation such Nation may have to the Organization. Any residual balance shall be refunded to the withdrawing Nation under such terms and conditions as the Conference may determine.

6.7 Voluntary contributions, whether or not in cash, may be accepted by the Director-General, and Trust and Special Funds may be established by him to cover moneys made available to the Organization for special purposes, provided that the purposes of such contributions and moneys are consistent with the policies, aims and activities of the Organization. The purposes and limits of any Trust and Special Funds shall be clearly defined. The acceptance of any such contributions and moneys which directly or indirectly involves additional fmancial obligations for Member Nations and Associate Members shall require the consent of the Conference. Trust and Special Funds and voluntary contributions shall be administered in accordance with the Financial Regulations of the Organization, unless otherwise provided for by the Conference. Trust and Special Funds shall be reported to the Finance Committee.

6.8 Reserve Funds may be established by the Conference.

6.9 There shall be established:

(*a*) an Information Products Revolving Fund to which shall be credited the proceeds of sales of information products and the revenue from advertising in and sponsorship of such products, except that where extrabudgetary funds are used to finance those information products, the proceeds of sales may be credited to such funds. The Fund shall be used only for the following purposes:

(*i*) to meet the direct costs of reproducing those information products for the sale of which there is a demand or reproducing new information products;

(*ii*) to pay, from within the resources available to the Fund, the direct costs, including costs of human resources and equipment, not covered by the Programme of Work and Budget, required for the sale and marketing of all such information products; and

(*iii*) to credit the originating divisions with such proportion of the proceeds credited to the Fund, up to 20 percent thereof, as may be determined by the Director-General, to be utilized within the biennium in which it is credited.

Any balance at the end of each financial period in excess of such sums as may be approved by the Finance Committee to cover commitments in respect of expenditures proposed by the Director-General for the following biennium shall be transferred to Miscellaneous Income.

(*b*) a Revolving Fund for FAO Products and Related Services other than Information Products to which shall be credited the proceeds of sales of such products as well as proceeds derived from licensing and other arrangements for their use, except that where extrabudgetary funds are used to finance the development of such products, such proceeds may be credited to such funds. The Fund shall be used only for the following purposes:

(*i*) to meet the direct costs of maintaining and further developing such products and making them widely available, and for developing new products;

(*ii*) to pay for direct costs of the production, sale and marketing of all such products, and protection of the property rights of these products.

Any balance at the end of each financial period in excess of such sums as may be approved by the Finance Committee to cover commitments in respect of expenditures proposed by the Director-General for the following biennium shall be transferred to Miscellaneous Income.

Regulation VII

Other income

7.1 Contributions from Associate Members and all receipts other than:

(*a*) contributions from Member Nations to the budget;

(*b*) direct refunds of expenditures made during the financial period;

(*c*) advances by Member Nations to the Working Capital Fund or deposits to Trust and Special Funds and other receipts directly related to those funds;

(*d*) proceeds of sales of information products and the revenue from advertising in and sponsorship of such products, and proceeds of sales of FAO products and related services, other than information products, developed by FAO, and proceeds derived from licensing and other arrangements for their use

shall be classed as Miscellaneous Income, for credit to the General Fund. Interest or other income derived from any Trust or Special Fund accepted by the Organization shall be credited to the fund to which it relates, unless provided for otherwise by the terms of the applicable Trust or Special Fund agreement.

7.2 Moneys accepted for purposes specified by the donor shall be treated as Trust or Special Funds under Regulation 6.7.

7.3 Moneys accepted in respect of which no purpose is specified shall be treated as Miscellaneous Income and reported as "Gifts" in the accounts of the General Fund.

7.4 Miscellaneous Income shall be estimated for each financial period. If the actual Miscellaneous Income for such period either exceeds or is less than the estimate, such excess or such shortfall shall form a part of the surplus or deficit of that financial period.

Regulation VIII

Custody of funds

8.1 The Director-General shall designate the bank or banks in which funds in the custody of the Organization shall be kept.

Regulation IX

Investment of funds

9.1 The Director-General may invest moneys not needed for immediate requirements seeking, wherever practicable, the advice of an Advisory Committee on Investments composed of not less than three and not more than five members appointed by the Director-General from persons outside the Organization having substantial experience in the financial sector. The investment of moneys standing to the credit of any Trust Fund, Reserve or Special Account shall be subject to any directives of the appropriate authority.

9.2 At least once a year the Director-General shall include in the financial statements submitted to the Finance Committee a statement of the investments currently held.

9.3 Income from investments shall be credited to the fund or account from which the invested moneys derive unless otherwise provided in the regulations, rules or resolutions relating to that fund or account.

Regulation X

Internal control

10.1 The Director-General shall:

(*a*) Establish detailed financial rules and procedures in order to ensure:

(*i*) effective financial administration and the exercise of economy; and

(*ii*) effective custody of the physical assets of the Organization;

(*b*) Except where advance or progress payments are specifically provided for in the contract, as may be required by normal commercial practice and the interests of the Organization, ensure that all payments are made on the basis of supporting vouchers and other documents which show that services or goods have been received and have not previously been paid for;

(*c*) Designate the officers, and other persons as appropriate, who may receive moneys, incur commitments or obligations and make payments on behalf of the Organization;

(*d*) Maintain an internal financial control and internal audit which shall provide an effective current examination and/or review of financial transactions in order to ensure:

(*i*) the regularity of the receipt, custody, and disbursement of all funds and other resources of the Organization;

(*ii*) the conformity of commitments or obligations and expenditures with the appropriations or other financial provisions voted by the Conference, or with the purposes, rules and provisions relating to the fund concerned; and

(*iii*) the economical use of the resources of the Organization.

10.2 Commitments or obligations shall not be incurred and payments shall not be made unless an appropriate authorization has been made in writing under the authority of the Director-General.

10.3 The Director-General may make such *ex gratia* payments as he deems to be necessary. A statement of such payments shall be submitted with the final accounts.

10.4 The Director-General may, after full investigation, authorize the writing off of losses of cash, supplies, equipment and other assets, other than arrears of contributions. A statement of all such losses written off during the financial period shall be submitted to the External Auditor with the final accounts.

10.5 The Director-General shall establish rules for the procurement of equipment, supplies and other requirements, including rules governing the invitation of tenders.

Regulation XI

The accounts

11.1 The Director-General shall maintain such accounts as are necessary and shall prepare final accounts for each financial period showing:

(*a*) The income and expenditure of all funds;

(*b*) The status of appropriations, including:

- (*i*) the original budget appropriations;
- (*ii*) any supplementary appropriations;
- (*iii*) the appropriations as modified by any transfers;
- (*iv*) credits, if any, other than the appropriations voted by the Conference; and
- (*v*) the amounts charged against the appropriations and against any other credits;

(*c*) Statements of assets and liabilities at the close of the financial period.

He shall also give such other information as may be necessary, to indicate the current financial position of the Organization.

11.2 Besides the final accounts for the financial period, the Director-General shall prepare, where the nature of the accounts so warrants, or in exceptional cases as decided by the Finance Committee, interim accounts at the end of each of the intervening years.

11.3 Appropriate separate accounts shall be maintained in respect of all trust funds, reserves and special accounts.

11.4 The final and any interim accounts of the Organization shall be presented in United States dollars. The accounting records may, however, be kept in such currency or currencies as the Director-General may deem necessary.

11.5 The final and any interim accounts shall be submitted to the External Auditor not later than 31 March following the end of the period to which they relate.

Regulation XII

External audit

Appointment

12.1 An External Auditor, who shall be the Auditor-General (or person exercising an equivalent function) of a Member Nation, shall be appointed in the manner and for the period decided by the Council.

Tenure of office

12.2 If the External Auditor ceases to hold the office of Auditor General (or equivalent function) in his own country, his tenure of office as External Auditor shall thereupon be terminated and he shall be succeeded as External Auditor by his successor as Auditor-General. The External Auditor may not otherwise be removed during his tenure of office except by the Council.

Scope of audit

12.3 The audit shall be conducted in conformity with generally accepted common auditing standards and, subject to any special directions of the Finance Committee, in accordance with the Additional Terms of Reference set out in Annex I to these Regulations.

12.4 The External Auditor may make observations with respect to the efficiency of the financial procedures, the accounting system, the internal financial controls and, in general, the administration and management of the Organization.

12.5 The External Auditor shall be completely independent and solely responsible for the conduct of the audit.

12.6 The Finance Committee may request the External Auditor to perform certain specific examinations and issue separate reports on the results.

Facilities

12.7 The Director-General shall provide the External Auditor with the facilities he may require in the performance of the audit.

12.8 For the purpose of making a local or special examination or of effecting economies of audit cost, the External Auditor may engage the services of any national Auditor-General (or person exercising an equivalent function) or commercial public auditors of known repute or any other person or firm who, in the opinion of the External Auditor, is technically qualified.

Reporting

12.9 The External Auditor shall issue a report on the audit of the financial statements and relevant schedules, which shall include such information as he deems necessary in regard to matters referred to in Financial Regulation 12.4 and in the Additional Terms of Reference.

12.10 The External Auditor's reports shall be transmitted through the Finance Committee, together with the audited financial statements, to the Council in accordance with any directions given by the Finance Committee. The Council shall examine the financial statements and the audit reports and shall forward them to the Conference with such comments as it deems advisable. The report on any interim accounts shall be submitted to the Finance Committee.

Regulation XIII

Resolutions involving expenditures

13.1 Before taking any decision involving expenditures, the Council or any commission or committee appointed by the Council or the Conference shall have before it a report from the Director-General on the administrative and financial implications of the proposals.

Regulation XIV

Delegation of authority

14.1 The Director-General may delegate to other officers of the Organization such authority as he considers necessary for the effective implementation of these Regulations.

Regulation XV

General provisions

15.1 These Regulations shall be effective from the beginning of the financial period following their approval by the Conference.

15.2 These Regulations may be amended by the Conference in the same manner as provided for amendments of the General Rules of the Organization (see Rule XLVIII).

Annex I

ADDITIONAL TERMS OF REFERENCE GOVERNING EXTERNAL AUDIT[1]

1. The External Auditor shall perform such audit of the accounts of the Organization, including all Trust Funds and special accounts, as he deems necessary in order to satisfy himself:

(*a*) that the financial statements are in accord with the books and records of the Organization;

(*b*) that the financial transactions reflected in the statements have been in accordance with the rules and regulations, the budgetary provisions and other applicable directives;

(*c*) that the securities and moneys on deposit and on hand have been verified by certificate received direct from the Organization's depositaries or by actual count;

(*d*) that the internal controls, including the internal audit, are adequate in the light of the extent of reliance placed thereon;

(*e*) that procedures satisfactory to the External Auditor have been applied to the recording of all assets, liabilities, surpluses and deficits.

2. The External Auditor shall be the sole judge as to the acceptance in whole or in part of certifications and representations by the Director-General and may proceed to such detailed examination and verification as he chooses of all financial records including those relating to supplies and equipment.

3. The External Auditor and his staff shall have free access at all convenient times to all books, records and other documentation which are, in the opinion of the External Auditor, necessary for the performance of the audit. Information classified as privileged and which the Director-General (or his designated senior official) agrees is required by the External Auditor for the purposes of the audit and information classified confidential shall be made available on application. The External Auditor and his staff shall respect the privileged and confidential nature of any information so classified which has been made available and shall not make use of it except in direct connection with the performance of the audit. The External Auditor may draw the attention of the Finance Committee to any denial of information classified as privileged which, in his opinion, was required for the purpose of the audit.

---

[1] See Financial Regulation 12.3.

4. The External Auditor shall have no power to disallow items in the accounts but shall draw to the attention of the Director-General for appropriate action any transaction concerning which he entertains doubt as to legality or propriety. Audit objections to these or any other transactions arising during the examination of the accounts shall be immediately communicated to the Director-General.

5. The External Auditor shall express and sign an opinion on the financial statements. The opinion shall include the following basic elements:

(*a*) the identification of the financial statements audited;

(*b*) a reference to the responsibility of the entity's management and the responsibility of the auditor;

(*c*) a reference to the audit standards followed;

(*d*) a description of the work performed;

(*e*) an expression of opinion on the financial statements as to whether:

- the financial statements present fairly the financial position as at the end of the period and the results of the operations for the period;
- the financial statements were prepared in accordance with the stated accounting policies; and
- the accounting policies were applied on a basis consistent with that of the preceding financial period;

(*f*) an expression of opinion on the compliance of transactions with the financial regulations and legislative authority;

(*g*) the date of the opinion;

(*h*) the external auditor's name and position; and

(*i*) should it be necessary, a reference to the report of the External Auditor on the financial statements.

6. The report of the External Auditor to the Conference on the financial operations of the period should mention:

(*a*) The type and scope of his examination.

(*b*) Matters affecting the completeness or accuracy of the accounts, including where appropriate:

(*i*) information necessary to the correct interpretation of the accounts;

(*ii*) any amounts which ought to have been received but which have not been brought to account;

(*iii*) any amounts for which a legal or contingent obligation exists and which have not been recorded or reflected in the financial statements;

(*iv*) expenditures not properly substantiated;

(*v*) whether proper books of accounts have been kept; where in the presentation of statements there are deviations of material nature from the generally accepted accounting principles applied on a consistent basis, these should be disclosed.

(*c*) Other matters which should be brought to the notice of the Finance Committee, such as:

(*i*) case of fraud or presumptive fraud;

(*ii*) wasteful or improper expenditure of the Organization's money or other assets (notwithstanding that the accounting for the transaction may be correct);

(*iii*) expenditure likely to commit the Organization to further outlay on a large scale;

(*iv*) any defect in the general system of detailed regulations governing the control of receipts and disbursements or of supplies and equipment;

(*v*) expenditure not in accordance with the intention of the Conference after making allowance for duly authorized transfers within the budget;

(*vi*) expenditure in excess of appropriations as amended by duly authorized transfers within the budget;

(*vii*) expenditure not in conformity with the authority which governs it.

(*d*) The accuracy or otherwise of the supplies and equipment records as determined by stocktaking and examination of the records.

In addition, the reports may contain reference to:

(*e*) Transactions accounted for in a previous year concerning which further information has been obtained or transactions in a later year concerning which it seems desirable that the Finance Committee should have early knowledge.

7. The External Auditor may make such observations with respect to his findings resulting from audit and such comments on the Director-General's financial report as he deems appropriate to the Finance Committee or to the Council or to the Director-General.

8. Whenever the External Auditor's scope of audit is restricted, or whenever he is unable to obtain sufficient evidence, the External Auditor shall refer to the matter in his opinion and report, making clear in the report the reasons for his comments, and the effect on the financial position and the financial transactions as recorded.

9. In no case shall the External Auditor include criticism in his report without first affording the Director-General an adequate opportunity of explanation on the matter under observation.

10. The External Auditor is not required to mention any matter referred to in the foregoing which, in his opinion, is insignificant in all respects.

RULES OF PROCEDURE OF THE COUNCIL OF FAO[1] /D

D

Rule I

Officers of the Council

1. The Council shall, at the beginning of each of its sessions, elect three Vice-Chairmen who shall remain in office until the election of new Vice-Chairmen at the next session of the Council.

2. The Chairman or, in the event of his absence and subject to the provisions of Rule XXIII.3 of the General Rules of the Organization, one of the Vice-Chairmen shall preside at meetings of the Council and exercise such other functions as are attributed to the Chairman by the General Rules of the Organization.

3. When in accordance with the provisions of Rule XXIII.3 of the General Rules of the Organization the Chairman of the Programme Committee acts as Chairman of the Council he shall, when presenting the Report of the Programme Committee to the Council, invite one of the Vice-Chairmen of the Council to take the chair.

4. In the absence from any meeting of the Chairman and the Vice-Chairmen, the Council shall appoint one of its Members to take the chair.

Rule II

Sessions

1. The Council shall hold sessions as provided for in Rule XXV of the General Rules of the Organization.

---

[1] Since the procedures of the Council of the Organization are already largely covered by the Constitution, the General Rules of the Organization and the Financial Regulations of the Organization, the Rules of Procedure adopted by the Council only supplement the foregoing provisions when required to facilitate the work of the Council.

2. As provided for in Rule XII.2 (*a*) of the General Rules of the Organization, the majority of the Members of the Council shall constitute a quorum, except as otherwise stipulated in the Constitution or the General Rules of the Organization.

3. Each session of the Council shall be held at the seat of the Organization unless, in pursuance of a previous decision of the Council or at the request of a majority of its Members, another place is designated.

4. Notice of the date of each session shall be communicated to all Member Nations and Associate Members of the Organization at least two months in advance of the session. In the case of great urgency this notice may be reduced to two weeks.

Rule III

Agenda

1. The first item on the provisional agenda of any session of the Council shall be the adoption of the agenda.

2. The provisional agenda for each session shall be communicated:

(*a*) to all Member Nations and Associate Members of the Organization, the United Nations, and such specialized agencies as have concluded formal agreements with the Organization;

(*b*) to such non-governmental organizations and such other international organizations as the Council may, from time to time, decide to invite to its sessions.

Rule IV

Voting

1. Voting in the Council shall be conducted in accordance with Rule XII of the General Rules of the Organization.

2. If the representative of a Member of the Council is serving as Chairman, the alternate or associate acting for him shall be permitted to participate in the proceedings and to vote in the Council.

Rule V

Committees

Committees may elect their own officers and determine their own procedures, except when otherwise specified.

Rule VI

Records and reports

1. Verbatim records shall be kept of all plenary meetings of the Council. The provisional verbatim records shall be circulated to all Members participating at the session in order to give them an opportunity to check the accuracy of the record of their interventions. The final version of the verbatim records shall be sent as soon as possible after the closure of the session to all Member Nations and Associate Members of the Organization.

2. The Director-General shall communicate, as soon as possible after the end of each regular session, a report embodying the text of all resolutions, recommendations, conventions, agreements, supplementary conventions or agreements, and of other formal decisions adopted or approved by the Council, including, when requested, a statement of minority views, to all Member Nations and Associate Members of the Organization, the United Nations, and the specialized agencies and non-governmental organizations with which the Organization has established relationship.

Rule VII

Expenses

1. The Director-General shall, in consultation with the Finance Committee, determine the actual allowances in conformity with the travel regulations of the Organization.

2. The respective governments shall be responsible for allowances of their representatives while in attendance at the meeting and, subject to Rule XXV.6 of the General Rules of the Organization, shall also be responsible for all travel and other expenses incurred by representatives, alternates, associates and advisers.

Rule VIII

Amendment of Rules

1. The Council may decide to amend its own Rules of Procedure, provided that such action is consistent with the Constitution and the General Rules of the Organization.

2. A Rule of Procedure of the Council may be suspended by the Council, provided that 24 hours' notice of the proposal for the suspension has been given. The notice may be waived if no member objects.

RULES OF PROCEDURE OF THE PROGRAMME COMMITTEE/E

Rule I

Officers

1. At the first session held during each calendar year the Committee shall elect a Vice-Chairman from among the representatives of its Members who shall remain in office until the election of a new Vice-Chairman at the first session in the next calendar year; the Vice-Chairman's term of office shall in any event terminate at the end of the Committee's term of office. If the Vice-Chairman is prevented from exercising his functions for the remainder of his term of office, due to resignation, disability, death or for any other reason, the Committee shall elect a new Vice-Chairman from among the representatives of its Members for the remainder of the Vice-Chairman's term of office.

2. The Chairman or, in his absence, the Vice-Chairman shall preside at meetings of the Committee and exercise such other functions as may be required to facilitate its work. In the absence from any meeting of the Chairman and Vice-Chairman, the Committee shall elect one of the representatives of its Members to take the chair.

3. If the Chairman of the Committee is prevented from exercising his functions for the remainder of his term of office, due to resignation, disability, death, or for any other reason, his functions shall be assumed by the Vice-Chairman for the remainder of the Chairman's term of office. The Committee shall elect a new Vice-Chairman from among the representatives of its Members for the remainder of the Vice-Chairman's term of office.

Rule II

Sessions and meetings

1. The Committee shall hold sessions as provided in Rule XXVI, paragraph 8 of the General Rules of the Organization.

2. (*a*) At the session or sessions held by the Committee in the first year of the biennium, the Committee shall:

(*i*) review the current activities of the Organization and the programme aspects of the current United Nations Development Programme;

(*ii*) consider the long-term programme objectives of the Organization in the light of the suggestions of the Conference, of the commissions and technical committees of the Conference, and of regional and other technical conferences.

(*b*) At the sessions held by the Programme Committee in the second year of the biennium, the Committee shall review:

(*i*) the summary and draft Programme of Work submitted by the Director-General for the following biennium, and the relevant financial aspects of the programme, particularly with regard to:

- content and balance of the programme, having regard to the extent to which it is proposed that existing activities be expanded, reduced in scope or discontinued;
- the extent of coordination of work between the different technical divisions of the Organization and between the Organization and other international organizations;
- the priorities to be given to existing activities, extension of such activities, and to new activities;

(*ii*) the programme aspects of the current United Nations Development Programme.

(*c*) The Programme Committee shall also consider at any of its sessions any item that may have been referred to it by the Council or the Director-General.

3. Any number of separate meetings may be held during each session of the Committee.

4. The meetings of the Committee shall be held in private, unless otherwise determined by the Committee.

5. The sessions of the Committee shall be held at the seat of the Organization or at another place, in pursuance of a decision of the Council.

6. Notice of the date and place of each session shall be communicated to all Members of the Committee and to their appointed representatives as early as possible in advance of the session.

7. If the representative of a Member of the Committee is expected to be unable to attend one full session, or if due to incapacity, death or any other reason he is prevented from exercising his functions for the remainder of the term for which the Member he represents has been elected, that Member shall inform the Director-General and the Chairman as soon as possible, and may designate a substitute representative who shall have the qualifications and experience referred to in paragraph 1 of Rule XXVI of the General Rules of the Organization.

8. The representatives of six Members shall constitute a quorum.

Rule III

Agenda

1. The Director-General, in consultation with the Chairman of the Committee, shall prepare a provisional agenda for any session of the Committee. Every effort shall be made to circulate to all Members of the Committee and to their appointed representatives, as early as possible in advance of that session, the agenda and the documents to be used by the Committee at that session.

2. The first item on the provisional agenda after the election of the Vice-Chairman shall be the adoption of the agenda.

3. Any Member of the Committee may request the Director-General to insert an item in the provisional agenda. The Director-General shall thereupon circulate the proposed item, together with any necessary papers, to all Members of the Committee and to their appointed representatives.

4. The Committee in session may amend the agenda by the deletion, addition, or modification of any item, provided that no matter referred to it by the Council or on the request of the Conference be omitted from the agenda as adopted.

Rule IV

Voting and proceedings

1. Each representative of a Member of the Committee, including the Chairman, shall have one vote.

2. Decisions of the Committee shall be taken by a majority of the votes cast.

3. For the conduct of the business of the Committee guidance may be sought from the relevant provisions of Rule XII of the General Rules of the Organization.

Rule V

Records and reports

1. At each session the Committee shall approve a report embodying its views, recommendations and decisions, including, when requested, a statement of minority views. Such other records for its own use as the Committee may on occasion decide shall also be maintained.

2. Where necessary, appropriate arrangements will be made for safeguarding the confidential nature of documents used by the Committee.

Rule VI

Expenses

1. The travelling expenses of the representative of each Member of the Committee properly incurred in travelling, by the most direct route, from the representative's duty station, to the site of the Committee session and return to his duty station, shall be borne by the Organization. Representatives of Members whose official work station is outside the site of the Committee's session shall also be paid a subsistence allowance while attending sessions of the Committee.

2. Travelling expenses and subsistence allowances shall be payable in accordance with the travel regulations of the Organization.

Rule VII

Suspension of Rules

A Rule of Procedure of the Committee may be suspended by the Committee, provided that 24 hours' notice of the proposal for the suspension has been given. Such notice may be waived if no representative of a Member objects.

RULES OF PROCEDURE OF THE FINANCE COMMITTEE/F

Rule I

Officers

1. At the first session held during each calendar year, the Committee shall elect a Vice-Chairman from among the representatives of its Members who shall remain in office until the election of a new Vice-Chairman at the first session in the next calendar year; the Vice-Chairman's term of office shall in any event terminate at the end of the Committee's term of office. If the Vice-Chairman is prevented from exercising his functions for the remainder of his term of office, due to resignation, disability, death or for any other reason the Committee shall elect a new Vice-Chairman from among the representatives of its Members for the remainder of the Vice-Chairman's term of office.

2. The Chairman or, in his absence, the Vice-Chairman shall preside at meetings of the Committee and exercise such other functions as may be required to facilitate its work. In the absence from any meeting of the Chairman and Vice-Chairman, the Committee shall elect one of the representatives of its Members to take the chair.

3. If the Chairman of the Committee is prevented from exercising his functions for the remainder of his term of office, due to resignation, disability, death, or for any other reason, his functions shall be assumed by the Vice-Chairman for the remainder of the Chairman's term of office. The Committee shall elect a new Vice-Chairman from among the representatives of its Members for the remainder of the Vice-Chairman's term of office.

Rule II

Sessions and meetings

1. (*a*) The Committee shall hold sessions as provided in Rule XXVII, paragraph 8 of the General Rules of the Organization.

(*b*) Where the required number of requests for the calling of a session of the Committee is received under Rule XXVII.8 (*a*) or (*b*) of the General Rules of the Organization and such requests indicate that the session should be called on a specified date or within a specified time limit, the Chairman and the Director-General shall consult each other and the Members of the Committee with a view to the calling of the session on the date or within the time limit specified, bearing in mind the pertinent factors, including the context and urgency of the request, the availability of the Chairman and the majority of the Members of the Committee, conflicting meeting schedules and the preparations necessary for convening the session.

(*c*) Any session called pursuant to such requests shall be called as soon as possible and at the latest within a period which shall not exceed 50 days from the date of receipt of the third request under subparagraph (*a*) or the fifth request under subparagraph (*b*) of Rule XXVII.8 of the General Rules of the Organization.

2. Any number of separate meetings may be held during each session of the Committee.

3. The meetings of the Committee shall be held in private, unless otherwise determined by the Committee.

4. The sessions of the Committee shall be held at the seat of the Organization or at another place, in pursuance of a decision of the Council.

5. Notice of the date and place of each session shall be communicated to all Members of the Committee and to their appointed representatives as early as possible in advance of the session.

6. If the representative of a Member of the Committee is expected to be unable to attend one full session, or if due to incapacity, death or any other reason he is prevented from exercising his functions for the remainder of the term for which the Member he represents has been elected, that Member shall inform the Director-General and the Chairman as soon as possible, and may designate a substitute representative who shall have the qualifications and experience referred to in paragraph 1 of Rule XXVII of the General Rules of the Organization.

7. The representatives of five Members shall constitute a quorum.

Rule III

Agenda

1. The Director-General, in consultation with the Chairman of the Committee, shall prepare a provisional agenda for any session of the Committee. Every effort shall be made to circulate to all Members of the Committee and to their appointed representatives, as early as possible in advance of that session, the agenda and the documents to be used by the Committee at that session.

2. The first item on the provisional agenda shall be the adoption of the agenda.

3. Any Member of the Committee may request the Director-General to insert an item in the provisional agenda. The Director-General shall there upon circulate the proposed item, together with any necessary papers, to all Members of the Committee and to their appointed representatives.

4. The Committee in session may amend the agenda by the deletion, addition, or modification of any item, provided that no matter referred to it by the Council or on the request of the Conference be omitted.

Rule IV

Voting

1. Each representative of a Member of the Committee, including the Chairman, shall have one vote.

2. Decisions of the Committee shall be taken by a majority of the votes cast.

3. Upon the request of any representative of a Member, voting shall be by roll call, in which case the vote of each representative shall be recorded.

4. When the Committee so decides, voting shall be by secret ballot.

5. In addition to the above Rules, the provisions of Rule XII of the General Rules of the Organization shall apply.

Rule V

Records and reports

1. At each session, the Committee shall approve a report embodying its views, recommendations and decisions, including, when requested, a statement of minority views. Such other records for its own use as the Committee may on occasion decide shall also be maintained.

2. Where necessary, appropriate arrangements will be made by the Committee for safeguarding the confidential nature of documents used in its deliberations.

Rule VI

Expenses

1. The travelling expenses of the representative of each Member of the Committee properly incurred in travelling, by the most direct route, from the representative's duty station, to the site of the Committee session and return to his duty station, shall be borne by the Organization. Representatives of Members whose official work station is outside the site of the Committee's session shall also be paid a subsistence allowance while attending sessions of the Committee.

2. Travelling expenses and subsistence allowances shall be payable in accordance with the travel regulations of the Organization.

Rule VII

Suspension of Rules

A Rule of Procedure of the Committee may be suspended by the Committee, provided that 24 hours' notice of the proposal for the suspension has been given. Such notice may be waived if no representative of a Member objects.

RULES OF PROCEDURE OF THE COMMITTEE ON COMMODITY PROBLEMS/G

G

Rule I

Officers

1. At the first session in each biennium, the Committee shall elect a Chairman, a first Vice-Chairman and a second Vice-Chairman from among the representatives of its Members, who shall remain in office until the election of a new Chairman and new Vice-Chairmen.

2. The Chairman, or in his absence one of the Vice-Chairmen, shall preside at meetings of the Committee and exercise such other functions as may be required to facilitate its work. In the event of the Chairman and the Vice-Chairmen not being able to preside at a meeting, the Committee shall appoint one of its Members to take the chair.

3. The Director-General of the Organization shall appoint a secretary, who shall perform such duties as the work of the Committee may require.

Rule II

Sessions

1. The Committee shall hold sessions as provided in Rule XXIX.4 and 5 of the General Rules of the Organization.

2. The Committee shall normally hold two sessions during each biennium, to be convened by the Director-General in consultation with the Chairman of the Committee, taking into account any proposals made by the Committee.

3. Any number of separate meetings may be held during each session of the Committee.

4. The sessions of the Committee shall normally be held at the seat of the Organization. A session may be held at another place in pursuance of a decision taken by the Committee in consultation with the Director-General or a request submitted in writing to the Director-General by a majority of the Members of the Committee.

5. Notice of the date and place of each session shall normally be communicated at least two months in advance of the session to all Member Nations and Associate Members of the Organization, and to such non-member States and international organizations as may have been invited to attend the session.

6. Each Member of the Committee may appoint alternates and advisers to its representative on the Committee.

7. Presence of representatives of a majority of the Members of the Committee shall constitute a quorum for any formal action by the Committee.

Rule III

Attendance

1. Participation of international organizations in an observer capacity in the work of the Committee shall be governed by the relevant provisions of the Constitution and the General Rules of the Organization,[1] as well as by the general rules of the Organization on relations with international organizations.

2. Attendance by non-member States of the Organization at sessions of the Committee shall be governed by the principles relating to the granting of observer status to nations adopted by the Conference.

3. (*a*) Meetings of the Committee shall be held in public, unless the Committee decides to meet in private for discussion of any items on its agenda.

(*b*) Subject to the provisions of subparagraph (*c*) below, any Member

[1] It is understood that in this context the terms "Constitution" and "the General Rules of the Organization" are to be taken to include all general rules and policy statements formally adopted by the Conference and intended to supplement the Constitution and the Rules, such as the "Statement of principles relating to the granting of observer status to nations", and the general rules regarding relationships between the Organization and governmental and non-governmental organizations.

Nation not represented on the Committee, any Associate Member or any non-member nation invited to attend in an observer capacity a session of the Committee may submit memoranda and participate without vote in any discussion at a public or private meeting of the Committee.

(*c*) In exceptional circumstances, the Committee may decide to restrict attendance at private meetings to the representative or observer of each Member Nation of the Organization.

Rule IV

Agenda and documents

1. The Director-General, in consultation with the Chairman of the Committee, shall prepare a provisional agenda and shall normally circulate it at least two months in advance of the session to all Member Nations and Associate Members of the Organization and to all international organizations invited to attend the session.

2. All Member Nations of the Organization and Associate Members acting within the limits of their status may request the Director-General normally not less than 30 days before the proposed date of the session to insert an item in the provisional agenda. The Director-General shall thereupon circulate the proposed item to all Members of the Committee, together with any necessary papers.

3. The first item on the provisional agenda shall be the adoption of the agenda. The Committee in session may by general consent amend the agenda by the deletion, addition or modification of any item, provided that no matter referred to it by the Council or on the request of the Conference may be omitted from the agenda.

4. Documents not already circulated shall be dispatched with the provisional agenda, or as soon as possible thereafter.

Rule V

Voting

1. Each Member of the Committee shall have one vote.

2. The decisions of the Committee shall be ascertained by the Chairman, who shall resort, upon the request of one or more Members, to a vote, in which case the pertinent provisions of Rule XII of the General Rules of the Organization shall apply *mutatis mutandis*.

Rule VI

Records and reports

1. At each session, the Committee shall approve a report to the Council embodying its views, recommendations and decisions, including, when requested, a statement of minority views. Any recommendation adopted by the Committee which affects the programme or finances of the Organization or concerning legal or constitutional matters shall be reported to the Council with the comments of the appropriate subsidiary committees of the Council.

2. Reports of sessions shall be circulated to all Member Nations and Associate Members of the Organization and to non-member States invited to attend the session, as well as to interested international organizations entitled to be represented at the session.

3. The comments of the Committee on the report of any of its subsidiary bodies and, if one or more Members of the Committee so request, the views of those Members shall be incorporated into the Committee's report. If any Member so requests, this part of the Committee's report shall be circulated as soon as possible by the Director-General to the States or international organizations which normally receive the reports of the subsidiary body in question. The Committee may also request the Director-General, in transmitting the report and records of its proceedings to Members, to call particular attention to its views and comments on the report of any of its subsidiary bodies.

4. Whenever a private meeting of the Committee is held, the Committee shall, at the beginning of that meeting, decide whether a record of the meeting shall be kept and, if so, what circulation, not exceeding that provided for in paragraph 2 above, shall be given to it.

5. The Committee shall determine the procedures in regard to press communiqués concerning its activities.

Rule VII

Subsidiary bodies

1. In accordance with the provisions of Rule XXIX.10 of the General Rules of the Organization, the Committee may, when necessary, establish subcommittees, intergovernmental commodity groups and ad hoc subsidiary bodies, subject to the necessary funds being available in the relevant chapter of the approved budget of the Organization. It may include in the membership of such subcommittees and ad hoc subsidiary bodies, Member Nations that are not members of the Committee and Associate Members. Membership of intergovernmental commodity groups established by the Committee shall be open to all Member Nations and Associate Members of the Organization and the Council may admit to membership of such groups States which, while not Member Nations or Associate Members of the Organization, are members of the United Nations, any of its specialized agencies or the International Atomic Energy Agency.

2. Before taking any decision involving expenditure in connection with the establishment of subsidiary bodies, the Committee shall have before it a report from the Director-General on the administrative and financial implications thereof.

3. The Committee shall determine the terms of reference of its subsidiary bodies who shall report to the Committee. The reports of the subsidiary bodies shall be made available for information to all members of the subsidiary bodies concerned, all Member Nations and Associate Members of the Organization, non-member States invited to the sessions of the subsidiary bodies, and to interested international organizations entitled to attend such sessions.

Rule VIII

Suspension of Rules

The Committee may decide to suspend any of the foregoing Rules of Procedure, provided that 24 hours' notice of the proposal for the suspension has been given and that the action contemplated is consistent with the Constitution and the General Rules of the Organization. [1] Such notice may be waived if no Member objects.

---

[1] See footnote to Rule III, paragraph 1.

Rule IX

Amendment of Rules

The Committee may, by a two-thirds majority of the votes cast, amend its Rules of Procedure, provided that such amendment is consistent with the Constitution and the General Rules of the Organization. No proposal for the amendment of these Rules shall be included in the agenda of any session of the Committee unless notice thereof has been dispatched by the Director-General to Members of the Committee at least 30 days before the opening of the session.

RULES OF PROCEDURE OF THE COMMITTEE ON FISHERIES/H

Rule I

Officers

1. At the first session in each biennium, the Committee shall elect a Chairman, a first Vice-Chairman and four other Vice-Chairmen from among the representatives of its Members, who shall remain in office until the election of a new Chairman and new Vice-Chairmen and who will act as a Steering Committee during sessions.

2. The Chairman, or in his absence the first Vice-Chairman, shall preside at meetings of the Committee and exercise such other functions as may be required to facilitate its work. In the event of the Chairman and the first Vice-Chairman not being able to preside at a meeting, the Committee shall appoint one of the other Vice-Chairmen or, failing these, a representative of its Members to take the chair.

3. The Director-General of the Organization shall appoint a secretary, who shall perform such duties as the work of the Committee may require and prepare the records of the proceedings of the Committee.

Rule II

Sessions

1. The Committee shall hold sessions as provided in Rule XXX.4 and 5 of the General Rules of the Organization.

2. Any number of separate meetings may be held during each session of the Committee.

3. The sessions of the Committee shall in the years immediately following

a regular session of the Conference be held at the seat of the Organization; in other years they may be held in another place in pursuance of a decision taken by the Committee in consultation with the Director-General.

4. Notice of the date and place of each session shall normally be communicated at least two months in advance of the session to all Member Nations and Associate Members of the Organization, and to such non-member States and international organizations as may have been invited to attend the session.

5. Each Member of the Committee may appoint alternates and advisers to its representative on the Committee.

6. Presence of representatives of a majority of the Members of the Committee shall constitute a quorum for any formal action by the Committee.

Rule III

Attendance

1. Participation of international organizations in an observer capacity in the work of the Committee shall be governed by the relevant provisions of the Constitution and the General Rules of the Organization,[1] as well as by the general rules of the Organization on relations with international organizations.

2. Attendance by non-member States of the Organization at sessions of the Committee shall be governed by the principles relating to the granting of observer status to nations adopted by the Conference.

3. (*a*) Meetings of the Committee shall be held in public, unless the Committee decides to meet in private for discussion of any items on its agenda.

(*b*) Subject to the provisions of subparagraph (*c*) below, any Member Nation not represented on the Committee, any Associate Member or any non-member State invited to attend in an observer capacity a session of the Committee may submit memoranda and participate without vote in any discussion at a public or private meeting of the Committee.

---

[1] It is understood that in this context the terms "Constitution" and "the General Rules of the Organization" are to be taken to include all general rules and policy statements formally adopted by the Conference and intended to supplement the Constitution and the Rules, such as the "Statement of principles relating to the granting of observer status to nations", and the general rules regarding relationships between the Organization and governmental and non-governmental organizations.

(*c*) In exceptional circumstances, the Committee may decide to restrict attendance at private meetings to the representative or observer of each Member Nation of the Organization.

Rule IV

Agenda and documents

1. The Director-General, in consultation with the Chairman of the Committee, shall prepare a provisional agenda and shall normally circulate it at least two months in advance of the session to all Member Nations and Associate Members of the Organization and to all non-member States and international organizations invited to attend the session.

2. All Member Nations of the Organization and Associate Members acting within the limits of their status may request the Director-General normally not less than 30 days before the proposed date of the session to insert an item in the provisional agenda. The Director-General shall thereupon circulate the proposed item to all Members of the Committee, together with any necessary papers.

3. The first item on the provisional agenda shall be the adoption of the agenda. The Committee in session may by general consent amend the agenda by the deletion, addition or modification of any item, provided that no matter referred to it by the Council or on the request of the Conference be omitted from the agenda.

4. Documents not already circulated shall be dispatched with the provisional agenda, or as soon as possible thereafter.

Rule V

Voting

1. Each Member of the Committee shall have one vote.

2. The decisions of the Committee shall be ascertained by the Chairman, who shall resort, upon the request of one or more Members, to a vote, in which case the pertinent provisions of Rule XII of the General Rules of the Organization shall apply *mutatis mutandis.*

Rule VI

Records and reports

1. At each session, the Committee shall approve a report to the Council embodying its views, recommendations and decisions, including when requested a statement of minority views. Any recommendations adopted by the Committee which affect the programme or finances of the Organization shall be reported to the Council with the comments of the appropriate subsidiary committees of the Council.

2. Reports of sessions shall be circulated to all Member Nations and Associate Members of the Organization and to non-member States invited to attend the session, as well as to interested international organizations entitled to be represented at the session.

3. The comments of the Committee on the report of any of its subsidiary bodies and, if one or more Members of the Committee so request, the views of those Members shall be incorporated into the Committee's report. If any Member so requests, this part of the Committee's report shall be circulated as soon as possible by the Director-General to the States or international organizations which normally receive the reports of the subsidiary body in question. The Committee may also request the Director-General, in transmitting the report and records of its proceedings to Members, to call particular attention to its views and comments on the report of any of its subsidiary bodies.

4. The Committee shall determine the procedures in regard to press communiqués concerning its activities.

Rule VII

Subsidiary bodies

1. In accordance with the provisions of Rule XXX.10 of the General Rules of the Organization, the Committee may, when necessary, establish subcommittees, subsidiary working parties or study groups, subject to the necessary funds being available in the relevant chapter of the approved budget of the Organization, and may include in the membership of such subcommittees, subsidiary working parties or study groups Member Nations that are not Members of the Committee and Associate Members. The membership of such

subcommittees, subsidiary working parties and study groups established by the Committee may include States which, while not Member Nations or Associate Members of the Organization, are members of the United Nations, any of its specialized agencies or the International Atomic Energy Agency.

2. Before taking any decision involving expenditure in connection with the establishment of subsidiary bodies, the Committee shall have before it a report from the Director-General on the administrative and financial implications thereof.

3. The Committee shall determine the terms of reference of its subsidiary bodies, who shall report to the Committee. The reports of the subsidiary bodies shall be made available for information to all members of the subsidiary bodies concerned, all Member Nations and Associate Members of the Organization, non-member States invited to the sessions of the subsidiary bodies, and to interested international organizations entitled to attend such sessions.

Rule VIII

Suspension of Rules

The Committee may decide to suspend any of the foregoing Rules of Procedure, provided that 24 hours' notice of the proposal for the suspension has been given and that the action contemplated is consistent with the Constitution and the General Rules of the Organization.[1] Such notice may be waived if no Member objects.

Rule IX

Amendment of Rules

The Committee may, by a two-thirds majority of the votes cast, amend its Rules of Procedure, provided that such amendment is consistent with the Constitution and the General Rules of the Organization. No proposal for the amendment of these Rules shall be included in the agenda of any session of the Committee unless notice thereof has been dispatched by the Director-General to Members of the Committee at least 30 days before the opening of the session.

---

[1] See footnote to Rule III, paragraph 1.

RULES OF PROCEDURE OF THE COMMITTEE ON FORESTRY/I

Rule I

Officers

1. At the first session in each biennium, the Committee shall elect a Chairman, a first Vice-Chairman and five other Vice-Chairmen from among the representatives of its Members, who shall remain in office until the election of a new Chairman and new Vice-Chairmen and who will act as a Steering Committee during sessions.

2. The Chairman, or in his absence the first Vice-Chairman, shall preside at meetings of the Committee and exercise such other functions as may be required to facilitate its work. In the event of the Chairman and the first Vice-Chairman not being able to preside at a meeting, the Committee shall appoint one of the other Vice-Chairmen or, failing these, a representative of one of its Members to take the chair.

3. The Director-General of the Organization shall appoint a secretary, who shall perform such duties as the work of the Committee may require.

Rule II

Sessions

1. The Committee shall hold sessions as provided in Rule XXXI.3 and 4 of the General Rules of the Organization.

2. Sessions of the Committee shall normally be held once in each biennium, preferably early in non-Conference years. Sessions shall be convened by the Director-General in consultation with the Chairman of the Committee, taking into account any proposals made by the Committee.

3. Notice of the date and place of each session shall normally be communicated at least three months in advance of the session to all Member Nations and Associate Members of the Organization, and to such non-member States and international organizations as may have been invited to attend the session.

4. Each Member of the Committee may appoint alternates and advisers to its representative on the Committee.

5. Presence of representatives of a majority of the Members of the Committee shall constitute a quorum for any formal action by the Committee.

Rule III

Attendance

1. Participation of international organizations in an observer capacity in the work of the Committee shall be governed by the relevant provisions of the Constitution and the General Rules of the Organization,[1] as well as by the general rules of the Organization on relations with international organizations.

2. Attendance by non-member States of the Organization at sessions of the Committee shall be governed by the principles relating to the granting of observer status to nations adopted by the Conference.

3. (*a*) Meetings of the Committee shall be held in public, unless the Committee decides to meet in private for discussion of any items on its agenda.

(*b*) Subject to the provisions of subparagraph (*c*) below, any Member Nation not represented on the Committee, any Associate Member or any non-member State invited to attend in an observer capacity a session of the Committee may submit memoranda and participate without vote in any discussion at a public or private meeting of the Committee.

(*c*) In exceptional circumstances, the Committee may decide to restrict attendance at private meetings to the representative or observer of each Member Nation of the Organization.

---

[1] It is understood that in this context the terms "Constitution" and "the General Rules of the Organization" are to be taken to include all general rules and policy statements formally adopted by the Conference and intended to supplement the Constitution and the Rules, such as the "Statement of principles relating to the granting of observer status to nations", and the general rules regarding relationships between the Organization and governmental and non-governmental organizations.

Rule IV

Agenda and documents

1. The Director-General, in consultation with the Chairman of the Committee, shall prepare a provisional agenda and shall normally circulate it at least two months in advance of the session to all Member Nations and Associate Members of the Organization and to all non-member States and international organizations invited to attend the session.

2. All Member Nations and Associate Members of the Organization may request the Director-General normally not less than 30 days before the proposed date of the session to insert an item in the provisional agenda. The Director-General shall thereupon circulate the proposed item to all Members of the Committee, together with any necessary papers.

3. The Committee in session may by general consent amend the agenda by the deletion, addition or modification of any item, provided that no matter referred to it by the Council or on the request of the Conference be omitted from the agenda.

4. Documents not already circulated shall be dispatched with the provisional agenda, or as soon as possible thereafter.

Rule V

Voting

1. Each Member of the Committee shall have one vote.

2. The decisions of the Committee shall be ascertained by the Chairman, who shall resort, upon the request of one or more Members, to a vote, in which case the pertinent provisions of Rule XII of the General Rules of the Organization shall apply *mutatis mutandis*.

Rule VI

Records and reports

1. At each session, the Committee shall approve a report to the Council embodying its views, recommendations and decisions, including when requested a statement of minority views. Any recommendation adopted by the Committee which affects the programme or finances of the Organization or concerning legal or constitutional matters shall be reported to the Council with the comments of the appropriate subsidiary committees of the Council.

2. Reports of sessions shall be circulated to all Member Nations and Associate Members of the Organization and to non-member States invited to attend the session, as well as to interested international organizations entitled to be represented at the session.

3. The comments of the Committee on the report of any of its subsidiary bodies and, if one or more Members of the Committee so request, the views of those Members shall be incorporated into the Committee's report. If any Member so requests, this part of the Committee's report shall be circulated as soon as possible by the Director-General to the States or international organizations which normally receive the reports of the subsidiary body in question. The Committee may also request the Director-General, in transmitting the report and records of its proceedings to Members, to call particular attention to its views and comments on the report of any of its subsidiary bodies.

4. The Committee shall determine the procedures in regard to press communiqués concerning its activities.

Rule VII

Subsidiary bodies

1. In accordance with the provisions of Rule XXXI.10 of the General Rules of the Organization, the Committee may, when necessary, establish subcommittees, subsidiary working parties or study groups, subject to the necessary funds being available in the relevant chapter of the approved budget of the Organization, and may include in the membership of such subcommittees, subsidiary working parties or study groups Member Nations and Associate Members that are not Members of the Committee. The Council may admit to

membership of subcommittees, subsidiary working parties and study groups established by the Committee States which, while not Member Nations of the Organization, are members of the United Nations, any of its specialized agencies or the International Atomic Energy Agency.

2. Before taking any decision involving expenditure in connection with the establishment of subsidiary bodies, the Committee shall have before it a report from the Director-General on the administrative and financial implications thereof.

3. The Committees shall determine the terms of reference of its subsidiary bodies, who shall report to the Committee. The reports of the subsidiary bodies shall be made available for information to all members of the subsidiary bodies concerned, all Member Nations and Associate Members of the Organization, non-member States invited to the sessions of the subsidiary bodies, and to interested international organizations entitled to attend such sessions.

Rule VIII

Suspension of Rules

The Committee may decide to suspend any of the foregoing Rules of Procedure, provided that 24 hours' notice of the proposal for the suspension has been given and that the action contemplated is consistent with the Constitution and the General Rules of the Organization.[1] Such notice may be waived if no Member objects.

Rule IX

Amendment of Rules

The Committee may, by a two-thirds majority of the votes cast, amend its Rules of Procedure, provided that such amendment is consistent with the Constitution and the General Rules of the Organization. No proposal for the amendment of these Rules shall be included in the agenda of any session of the Committee, unless notice thereof has been dispatched by the Director-General to Members of the Committee at least 30 days before the opening of the session.

---

[1] See footnote to Rule III, paragraph 1.

RULES OF PROCEDURE OF THE COMMITTEE ON AGRICULTURE/J

Rule I

Officers

1. At the first session in each biennium, the Committee shall elect a Chairman, a first Vice-Chairman and a second Vice-Chairman from among the representatives of its Members, who shall remain in office until the election of a new Chairman and new Vice-Chairmen.

2. The Chairman, or in his absence one of the Vice-Chairmen, shall preside at meetings of the Committee and exercise such other functions as may be required to facilitate its work. In the event of the Chairman and the Vice-Chairmen not being able to preside at a meeting, the Committee shall appoint a representative of one of its Members to take the chair.

Rule II

Sessions

1. The Committee shall hold sessions as provided in Rule XXXII.3 and 4 of the General Rules of the Organization.

2. Any number of separate meetings may be held during each session of the Committee.

3. Sessions of the Committee shall normally be held once in each biennium, preferably early in Conference years. Sessions shall be convened by the Director-General in consultation with the Chairman of the Committee taking into account any proposals made by the Committee.

4. If required, the Committee may hold additional sessions on the call of the Director-General in consultation with its Chairman, or on request submit-

ted in writing to the Director-General by the majority of the Members of the Committee.

5. Notice of the date and place of each session shall normally be communicated at least two months in advance of the session to all Member Nations and Associate Members of the Organization, and to such non-member States and international organizations as may have been invited to attend the session.

6. Each Member of the Committee may appoint alternates, associates and advisers to its representative on the Committee.

7. Presence of representatives of a majority of the Members of the Committee shall constitute a quorum for any formal action by the Committee.

Rule III

Attendance

1. Participation of international organizations in an observer capacity in the work of the Committee shall be governed by the relevant provisions of the Constitution and the General Rules of the Organization,[1] as well as by the general rules of the Organization on relations with international organizations.

2. Attendance by non-member States of the Organization at sessions of the Committee shall be governed by the principles relating to the granting of observer status to nations adopted by the Conference.

3. (*a*) Meetings of the Committee shall be held in public, unless the Committee decides to meet in private for discussion of any items on its agenda.

(*b*) Subject to the provisions of subparagraph (*c*) below, any Member Nation not represented on the Committee, any Associate Member or any non-member State invited to attend in an observer capacity a session of the Committee may submit memoranda and participate without vote in any discussion at a public or private meeting of the Committee.

[1] It is understood that in this context the terms "Constitution" and "the General Rules of the Organization" are to be taken to include all general rules and policy statements formally adopted by the Conference and intended to supplement the Constitution and the Rules, such as the "Statement of principles relating to the granting of observer status to nations", and the general rules regarding relationships between the Organization and governmental and non-governmental organizations.

(*c*) In exceptional circumstances, the Committee may decide to restrict attendance at private meetings to the representative or observer of each Member Nation of the Organization.

Rule IV

Agenda and documents

1. The Director-General, in consultation with the Chairman of the Committee, shall prepare a provisional agenda and shall normally circulate it at least two months in advance of the session to all Member Nations and Associate Members of the Organization and to all non-member States and international organizations invited to attend the session.

2. All Member Nations of the Organization and Associate Members may request the Director-General normally not less than 30 days before the proposed date of the session to insert an item in the provisional agenda. The Director-General shall thereupon circulate the proposed item to all Members of the Committee, together with any necessary papers.

3. The Committee in session may by general consent amend the agenda by the deletion, addition or modification of any item, provided that no matter referred to it by the Council or on request of the Conference be omitted from the agenda.

4. Documents not already circulated shall be dispatched with the provisional agenda, or as soon as possible thereafter.

Rule V

Voting

1. Each Member of the Committee shall have one vote.

2. The decisions of the Committee shall be ascertained by the Chairman, who shall resort, upon the request of one or more Members, to a vote, in which case the pertinent provisions of Rule XII of the General Rules of the Organization shall apply *mutatis mutandis*.

Rule VI

Reports

1. At each session, the Committee shall approve a report embodying its views, recommendations and decisions, including, when requested, a statement of minority views. Any recommendations adopted by the Committee which affect the programme or finances of the Organization or concerning legal or constitutional matters shall be reported to the Council with the comments of the appropriate subsidiary committees of the Council. The reports of the Committee shall also be placed before the Conference.

2. Reports of sessions shall be circulated to all Member Nations and Associate Members of the Organization and to non-member States invited to attend the session, as well as to interested international organizations entitled to be represented at the session.

3. The comments of the Committee on the report of any of its subsidiary bodies and, if one or more Members of the Committee so request, the views of those Members shall be incorporated into the Committee's report. If any Member so requests, this part of the Committee's report shall be circulated as soon as possible by the Director-General to the States or international organizations which normally receive the reports of the subsidiary body in question. The Committee may also request the Director-General, in transmitting the report and records of its proceedings to Members, to call particular attention to its views and comments on the report of any of its subsidiary bodies.

4. The Committee shall determine the procedures in regard to press communiqués concerning its activities.

Rule VII

Subsidiary bodies

1. In accordance with Rule XXXII.12 of the General Rules of the Organization, the Committee may, on an exceptional basis, establish subsidiary or ad hoc bodies where it considers that such action is conducive to facilitating its own work and will not adversely affect the multidisciplinary consideration of questions submitted to the Committee for examination. The Committee may include in the membership of such subsidiary or ad hoc bodies Member

Nations that are not Members of the Committee and Associate Members. The Council may admit to membership of such subsidiary or ad hoc bodies established by the Committee States which, while not Member Nations or Associate Members of the Organization, are members of the United Nations, any of its specialized agencies or the International Atomic Energy Agency.

2. Before taking a decision on the establishment of any subsidiary or ad hoc body, the Committee shall examine the administrative and financial implications of such a decision, in the light of a report to be submitted by the Director-General.

3. The Committee shall define the terms of reference, composition and, as far as possible, the duration of the mandate of each subsidiary or ad hoc body. Such subsidiary or ad hoc bodies shall report to the Committee. The reports of the subsidiary or ad hoc bodies shall be made available for information to all members of the subsidiary or ad hoc bodies concerned, all Member Nations and Associate Members of the Organization, non-member States invited to the session of the subsidiary or ad hoc bodies, and to interested international organizations entitled to attend such sessions.

Rule VIII

Suspension of Rules

The Committee may, by a two-thirds majority of the votes cast, decide to suspend any of the foregoing Rules of Procedure, provided that 24 hours' notice of the proposal for the suspension has been given and that the action contemplated is consistent with the Constitution and the General Rules of the Organization.[1] Such notice may be waived if no Member objects.

Rule IX

Amendment of Rules

The Committee may, by a two-thirds majority of the votes cast, amend its Rules of Procedure, provided that such amendment is consistent with the Constitution and the General Rules of the Organization. No proposal for the

[1] See footnote to Rule III, paragraph 1.

amendment of these Rules shall be included in the agenda of any session of the Committee, unless notice thereof has been dispatched by the Director-General to Members of the Committee at least 30 days before the opening of the session.

RULES OF PROCEDURE OF THE COMMITTEE ON WORLD FOOD SECURITY/K

Rule I

Membership

Membership of the Committee shall be in accordance with Rule XXXIII.1 of the General Rules of the Organization.

Rule II

Officers

1. At the first session of the Committee held after a regular session of the Conference, the Committee shall elect a Chairman and four Vice-Chairmen from among the representatives of its Members, who shall remain in office until the election of a new Chairman and new Vice-Chairmen. The Chairman and Vice-Chairmen shall not be eligible for election for two consecutive terms in the same office.

2. The Chairman, or in his absence one of the Vice-Chairmen, shall preside at meetings of the Committee and exercise such other functions as may be required to facilitate its work. In the event of the Chairman and the Vice-Chairmen not being able to preside at a meeting, the Committee shall appoint a representative of one of its Members to take the chair.

Rule III

Secretary

The Director-General of the Organization shall appoint a Secretary who shall perform such duties as the work of the Committee may require.

Rule IV

Sessions

1. The Committee shall hold sessions as provided in Rule XXXIII.3 and 4 of the General Rules of the Organization, and shall propose the date and place of its sessions.

2. Any number of separate meetings may be held during each session of the Committee.

3. Notice of the date and place of each session shall normally be communicated at least two months in advance of the session to all Member Nations and Associate Members of the Organization, to all Member States of the United Nations and to such international organizations as may have been invited to attend the session.

4. Each Member of the Committee may appoint alternates, associates and advisers to its representative on the Committee.

5. Presence of representatives of a majority of the Members of the Committee shall constitute a quorum for any formal action by the Committee.

Rule V

Attendance

1. Any Member Nation of the Organization or Member State of the United Nations not represented on the Committee, any Associate Member or any State that is not a member of the Organization or of the United Nations but a member of a specialized agency or of the International Atomic Energy Agency, or liberation movements in accordance with decisions of the Conference and Council, may attend in an observer capacity a session of the Committee and may submit memoranda and participate without vote in any discussions at a public or private meeting of the Committee.

2. Participation of international organizations, non-governmental organizations and other actors of civil society in an observer capacity in the work of the Committee shall be governed by the relevant provisions of the Constitution and the General Rules of the Organization, as well as by the rules of the

Organization on relations with international organizations, taking into account the provisions of Rule XXXIII of the General Rules of the Organization.

3. In accordance with Rule XXXIII.12 of the General Rules of the Organization, relevant international organizations shall be invited to participate in the work of the Committee and the preparation of meeting documents on matters within their respective mandates in collaboration with the secretariat of the Committee.

4. Meetings of the Committee shall be held in public, unless the Committee decides to meet in private for discussion of any items on its agenda.

Rule VI

Agenda and documents

1. The Director-General, in consultation with the Chairman of the Committee, shall prepare a provisional agenda and shall normally circulate it at least three months in advance of the session to all Member Nations and Associate Members of the Organization, to all Member States of the United Nations and to all international organizations invited to attend the session.

2. All Member Nations and Associate Members of the Organization and all non-member States which are members of the Committee may request the Director-General, normally not less than 30 days before the proposed date of the session, to insert an item in the provisional agenda. The Director-General shall thereupon circulate the proposed item to all Members of the Committee, together with any necessary papers.

3. The Committee in session may, by a two-thirds majority of the votes cast, amend the agenda by the deletion, addition or modification of any item, provided that no matter referred to it by the Council or on request of the Conference be omitted from the agenda.

4. Documents which have not already been dispatched shall be dispatched with the provisional agenda or as soon as possible thereafter in all the languages of the Organization.

Rule VII

Voting

1. Each Member of the Committee shall have one vote.

2. The decisions of the Committee shall be ascertained by the Chairman, who shall resort, upon the request of one or more Members, to a vote, in which case the pertinent provisions of Rule XII of the General Rules of the Organization shall apply *mutatis mutandis*.

Rule VIII

Reports

1. At each session, the Committee shall approve a report embodying its views, recommendations and decisions, including, when requested, a statement of minority views. Any recommendations adopted by the Committee which affect the programme or finances of the Organization or concerning legal or constitutional matters shall be reported to the Council with the comments of the appropriate subsidiary committees of the Council.

2. Reports of sessions shall be submitted to the Council and circulated to all Member Nations and Associate Members of the Organization, and to those non-member States which are Members of the Committee, as well as to interested international and non-governmental organizations entitled to be represented at the session.

3. Pursuant to Rule XXXIII.9 of the General Rules of the Organization, the Committee shall provide regular reports to the Economic and Social Council of the United Nations (ECOSOC), through the Council of the Organization.

Rule IX

Subsidiary bodies

1. In accordance with Rule XXXIII.16 of the General Rules of the Organization, the Committee may establish subsidiary or ad hoc bodies where it

considers that such action would expedite its own work, without duplicating the work of existing bodies.

2. Before taking a decision on the establishment of any subsidiary or ad hoc body, the Committee shall examine the administrative and financial implications of such a decision, in the light of a report to be submitted by the Director-General.

3. The Committee shall define the terms of reference, composition and, as far as possible, the duration of the mandate of each subsidiary or ad hoc body. Such subsidiary or ad hoc bodies shall report to the Committee. The reports of the subsidiary or ad hoc bodies shall be made available for information to all members of the subsidiary or ad hoc bodies concerned, all Members of the Committee, and to interested international organizations entitled to attend sessions of the bodies concerned.

Rule X

Suspension of Rules

The Committee may, by a two-thirds majority of the votes cast, decide to suspend any of the foregoing Rules of Procedure, provided that the action contemplated is consistent with the Constitution and the General Rules of the Organization and that 24 hours' notice of the proposal for the suspension has been given. Such notice may be waived if no Member objects.

Rule XI

Amendment of Rules

The Committee may, by a two-thirds majority of the votes cast, amend its Rules of Procedure provided that such amendment is consistent with the Constitution and the General Rules of the Organization. No proposal for the amendment of these Rules of Procedure shall be included in the agenda of any session of the Committee, unless notice thereof has been dispatched by the Director-General to Members of the Committee at least 30 days before the opening of the session.

VOLUME II

GRANTING OF OBSERVER STATUS (IN RESPECT OF NATIONS)/L

Granting of observer status[1]

1. At its eighth session the Conference requested the Council to consider and suggest amendments to the Constitution and General Rules of the Organization for the purpose of eliminating any possible ambiguity with respect to the question of observer status, with special reference to the definition of such status, the establishment of criteria for the granting of the status and the consideration of all juridical and practical aspects of the problem.

Observer status in respect of nations

2. The ninth session of the Conference accepted the Council's view that the objective would be fulfilled by defining (*a*) the categories of nations that may be invited to send observers to meetings of the Organization, (*b*) the authority that may grant the status of observer to such nations, and (*c*) the status to be accorded to observers; and that, since there were very few provisions in the Constitution and General Rules of the Organization relating to observer status in respect of nations, it was preferable to formulate a statement of principles[2] on the subject.

3. Therefore, after introducing certain amendments to the text which the Council had proposed (see Report of the twenty-sixth session of the Council), the Conference adopted the following Resolution:

---

[1] See paragraphs 497 to 499 of the *Report of the ninth session of the Conference*. As regards the granting of observer status in respect of international governmental and non-governmental organizations, see page 183.

[2] The reasons for the adoption of the various principles set out in the Resolution are fully explained in the *Report of the twenty-sixth session of the Council.*

RESOLUTION No. 43/57

Observer status in respect of nations

THE CONFERENCE

Considering *that Article III of the Constitution and the relevant General Rules of the Organization regarding observer status are not sufficiently clear;*

Adopts *the statement of principles relating to the granting of observer status to nations set forth in Appendix C to this report;*[1]

Requests *all bodies set up under the aegis of the Organization in accordance with Articles VI and XIV of the Constitution to bring their statutes and rules of procedure into harmony with the aforementioned principles at the earliest possible date.*

4. The Conference considered that the principles set out in Section A, paragraph 2 of the statement of principles referred to above should be included in the General Rules of the Organization and consequently requested the Council to submit to the next session of the Conference a draft amendment to Rule XXVI.9 (new Rule XXV.9).

[1] Appendix C to the *Report of the ninth session of the Conference* appears in this volume on pages 161 to 164.

Appendix[1]

STATEMENT OF PRINCIPLES RELATING TO THE GRANTING OF OBSERVER STATUS TO NATIONS

A. Member Nations and Associate Members

1. *Sessions of the Conference, Council, commissions and committees*

Member Nations and Associate Members of the Organization may not attend any session of the Conference in an observer capacity. This principle shall also apply to members of the Council and of the commissions and committees established under Article VI or Article XIV of the Constitution with respect to attendance at the sessions of such bodies.

2. *Executive, private or closed meetings of the Council*

Rule XXV.9 (*c*) of the General Rules of the Organization provides that any Member Nation not represented on the Council and any Associate Member may submit memoranda and participate without vote in any discussion of the Council. In interpreting this Rule it will be understood that, as a general practice, Member Nations of the Organization that are not members of the Council, or Associate Members, should be admitted to private meetings, unless the Council decides otherwise in cases of necessity.

3. *Regional or technical meetings (including those of regional commissions set up under Article VI of the Constitution)*

Any Member Nation or Associate Member may, on request, participate in the capacity of observer in any regional or technical meeting of the FAO governing or subsidiary bodies, or any regional or technical meeting of which the Director-General on the authority of the Council assumes the initiative or has the primary organizing responsibility, even though the Member Nation or Associate Member does not geographically belong to the particular region, always provided that the Member Nation or Associate Member has a definite interest in the subject matter to be discussed. Notice of the intention to

---

[1] Appendix C to the *Report of the ninth session of the Conference*.

attend any such meeting should be given to the Director-General at least 15 days before the meeting, it being understood that notice may be waived by the meeting itself.[1]

4. *Committees consisting of a limited number of Member Nations and Associate Members*

Committees consisting of a limited number of Member Nations and Associate Members established by the Conference or its commissions or by the Council, under Article VI of the Constitution, or Rules XIV, XV or XXV.10 of the General Rules of the Organization, shall not be open to attendance by observers of Member Nations or Associate Members that are not members of such committees unless otherwise determined by the Conference, the said commissions or the Council.

5. *Dependent territories of and trust territories administered by Member Nations*

The Director-General may draw the attention of a metropolitan power or administering authority to the desirability of its participation in a regional or technical meeting of interest to a particular dependent or trust territory.

B. Non-member States

1. States which, while not Member Nations or Associate Members of the Organization, are members of the United Nations, any of its specialized agencies or the International Atomic Energy Agency may, on request, and subject to the provisions of paragraph B.4, be invited by the Conference or the Council to be represented by an observer at a session of the Conference or Council.

2. Such non-member States may, on request and with the approval of the Council, attend regional or technical meetings of the Organization. In cases of urgency, however, where there is insufficient time to consult the Council, the Director-General may on request invite such non-member States to send an observer to such meetings.

---

[1] The position regarding bodies set up under Article XIV of the Constitution is covered in Appendix D of the *Report of the ninth session of the Conference* ("Principles and Procedures which should govern Conventions and Agreements concluded under Articles XIV and XV of the Constitution, and Commissions and Committees established under Article VI of the Constitution") which appears in this volume on pages 189 to 200.

3. States which are not Members or Associate Members of the Organization or members of the United Nations, any of its specialized agencies or the International Atomic Energy Agency shall not be permitted to send observers to any meeting of the Organization.

4. Former Member Nations of the Organization that have withdrawn leaving arrears of contributions shall not be permitted to send an observer to any meeting of the Organization until such time as they have paid up all such arrears or the Conference has approved an arrangement for the settlement thereof, or unless the Council, in special circumstances, decides otherwise with respect to such attendance.

5. Should an application for membership have been received by the Organization, the requesting authority may, subject to the provisions of the preceding paragraph 4, be invited by the Council to participate in an observer capacity in technical meetings, in which such authority is regarded as having a technical interest, pending a decision of the Conference on the application.

6. Rules XXIV.1 (*d*) (*v*) and XXXII.2[1] of the General Rules of the Organization shall be interpreted in the light of the principles laid down in paragraphs B.3 and B.4.

7. The occasion may arise when a non member of the Organization which is, however, a member of the United Nations, any of its specialized agencies or the International Atomic Energy Agency needs to be consulted, because of emergency conditions, on some technical action, in which case the restrictive nature of paragraphs B.4 and B.5 above should not debar the Director-General from inviting an observer from such non member to attend a technical meeting for the discussion on a particular subject, if he deems such an invitation to be in the best interests of the Organization and its work, on the understanding that the Director-General shall consult the Members of the Council, if necessary by correspondence.

C. Status of observers

1. Observers from nations admitted to meetings of the Organization may be permitted:

(1) to make only formal statements in Conference and Council plenaries and

[1] Now Rule XXXV.2.

in Commissions of the Whole, subject to the approval of the General Committee of the Conference, or of the Council;

(2) to participate in the discussions of the commissions and committees of the Conference and Council and in the discussions of technical meetings, subject to the approval of the Chairman of the particular meeting and without the right to vote;

(3) to receive the documents other than those of a restricted nature for and the report of the particular meeting;

(4) to submit written statements on particular items of the agenda;

(5) to attend a private meeting of the Council or of a commission or committee established by the Conference or Council, subject to the following rule:

When it is decided that the Council or a commission or committee established by the Conference or Council shall hold a private meeting, the Conference, Council, commission or committee, subject to the provisions of the Constitution and the General Rules of the Organization and to the principles laid down in the present Resolution, shall, at the same time, determine the scope of such a decision with respect to observers of Member Nations and Associate Members that are not members of the commission or committee and to observers of non-member nations that have been invited to be represented at the session of the commission or committee.

COOPERATION WITH INTERNATIONAL GOVERNMENTAL ORGANIZATIONS/M

Methods applied

1. The ninth session of the Conference[1] noted from the Council's report on this subject (C 57/37) that the methods applied in developing cooperation with the United Nations group of organizations were matters that were dealt with by consultations between the heads of the organizations concerned and came to be modified appropriately as circumstances demanded and opportunity arose.

2. Where there was an agreement or an exchange of letters between FAO and another international organization, the well-defined relationship was likely from time to time to be brought into line with changing conditions. The Committee on Commodity Problems kept itself regularly informed of the work of many specialized international non-governmental organizations in the commodity field. Thus methods of developing cooperation with such organizations were automatically under constant scrutiny.

3. In general, the Conference agreed with the Council that so far as intergovernmental organizations were concerned the emphasis should by and large be on a practical exchange of knowledge and ideas, exchange of appropriate selected documents and publications, joint action projects for which the respective organizations were suitably equipped and in which joint action, with appropriate allocation of functions, offered the best solution to the particular problem. The tendency with regard to attendance at meetings should be increasingly to keep participation to technical meetings or at most to meetings where technical policy was made and the question of relations discussed.

---

[1] See paragraphs 488 to 490 of the *Report of the ninth session of the Conference*.

GUIDING LINES REGARDING RELATIONSHIP AGREEMENTS BETWEEN FAO AND INTERGOVERNMENTAL ORGANIZATIONS/N

Preamble

1. The twenty-ninth session of the Council having before it the draft of an agreement between FAO and an intergovernmental organization requested the Committee on Constitutional and Legal Matters to examine the draft. The Committee in reporting to the thirty-first session of the Council drew attention to the fact that over the last several years a set of principles had been formulated and approved by the Conference governing relationship between FAO and international non-governmental organizations, but that no such principles had so far been established with respect to intergovernmental organizations and that in the absence of guiding principles the Committee experienced difficulty in carrying out its task.

2. The Council concurred with the view of the Committee that a set of criteria be drawn up which would serve as guiding lines in the light of which proposals regarding relationship agreements with intergovernmental organizations should be examined.

3. The tenth session of the Conference[1] had before it a set of guiding lines drawn up by the Committee on Constitutional and Legal Matters at the request of the Council and transmitted to the Conference as document C59/32.

4. Two Member Nations expressed the view that a more restrictive criterion should be adopted as to the objectives and activities of any intergovernmental organizations in the field of food and agriculture. It was the majority opinion, however, that there should not be any change in the criteria as drafted by the Committee on Constitutional and Legal Matters.

[1] See paragraphs 599 to 602 of the *Report of the tenth session of the Conference*.

RESOLUTION No. 69/59

Guiding lines regarding relationship between FAO and intergovernmental organizations

THE CONFERENCE

Noting *the absence of a set of established criteria regarding relationship between FAO and intergovernmental organizations;*

Considering *the desirability of adopting a set of guiding lines which should be taken into account when considering proposals for formal relationship agreements with intergovernmental organizations;*

Having examined *the guiding lines drawn up by the Committee on Constitutional and Legal Matters and transmitted to the Conference through the Council as document C59/32;*

Approves *these guiding lines, which should serve as a reminder of the points to be considered when examining formal relationship agreements between FAO and intergovernmental organizations, and the text of which is appended hereto as Appendix G.*[1]

---

[1] Appendix G of the *Report of the tenth session of the Conference* appears in this volume on pages 169 to 171.

Appendix[1]

GUIDING LINES FOR FORMAL RELATIONSHIP AGREEMENTS BETWEEN FAO AND OTHER INTERGOVERNMENTAL ORGANIZATIONS

Preamble

The following matters should be taken into account when considering relationship agreements with international intergovernmental organizations other than those of the United Nations family:

A. Intergovernmental character of the other organization.

B. Desirability of concluding formal agreements.

C. Contents of agreements – scope and method of cooperation.

A. Intergovernmental character of the other organization

The present criteria applied by FAO for recognizing the intergovernmental character of an organization should be maintained, i.e.:

(*a*) The organization should have been set up by an intergovernmental convention (a convention to which the parties are States).

(*b*) The governing body of the organization should be composed of members designated by governments.

(*c*) The income of the organization should be made up mainly, if not exclusively, of contributions from governments.

B. Desirability of concluding formal agreements

When taking a policy decision as to whether a focal agreement should be concluded with an intergovernmental organization, consideration should be given to:

1. *Factors inherent in the other organization*

(*a*) The aims and purposes of the organization should be in conformity with the general principles embodied in the Charter of the United Nations and the Constitution of FAO.

---

[1] Appendix G to the *Report of the tenth session of the Conference.*

(*b*) The objectives and activities of the organization should be related at least partly to food and agriculture and/or should have the purpose of promoting cooperation among the members of the organization in related fields.

(*c*) The structure and methods of operation of the organization should be such as to ensure that it may effectively cooperate with FAO and further the objectives of FAO.

(*d*) The organization should have legal capacity to enter into agreements with other international organizations; prior evidence should be obtained that the conclusion of an agreement has been duly authorized by the competent body.

(*e*) The nature of the relations that the organization has established with other intergovernmental organizations, including those of the United Nations family, should be taken into account.

(*f*) Agreements should be concluded only with organizations whose members are members of at least one of the organizations of the United Nations family, unless special circumstances would warrant a decision to the contrary.

2. *Factors relating to cooperation with FAO*

(*a*) The purpose of cooperation should be to provide for consultation, coordination of effort, mutual assistance and possibly joint action in fields of mutual interest on the understanding that cooperation is designed to further the objectives of FAO.

(*b*) The degree and extent of present, past and/or future cooperation with FAO should warrant the conclusion of a formal agreement.

(*c*) Consideration should be given to the question as to whether:

  (*i*) well-defined permanent arrangements are desirable to set out the bases of cooperation and to avoid duplication or for other reasons;

  (*ii*) an ad hoc regional arrangement instead of a formal agreement would as well serve the desired purpose; or

  (*iii*) difficulties have arisen in carrying out informal cooperation which could not be eliminated without the conclusion of a formal agreement.

(*d*) The administrative and financial implications of the agreement for FAO should be considered in consultation with the Programme and Finance Committees.

C. Contents of agreements – scope and method of cooperation

The provisions of the agreements should be consistent with those of the Constitution and Rules of the Organization, and be as specific as possible as to the forms of cooperation, and should not create operational or procedural difficulties which would outweigh the value of the agreement for the Organization.

Methods of *liaison* which should be considered are as follows:

(*a*) reporting on activities performed;

(*b*) right to suggest insertion of specific items in agenda of governing bodies;

(*c*) extent of reciprocal representation at meetings and arrangements therefor;

(*d*) exchange of publications and, as appropriate, of other forms of documentation.

Methods of close *cooperation* and avoidance of duplication should include:

(*a*) distribution of responsibilities;

(*b*) indication of specific fields in which cooperation is required;

(*c*) consultation at all stages of planning and execution of programmes of interest to either organization;

(*d*) nature and methods of joint action;

(*e*) cooperation for dissemination of information, including methods for financing such action;

(*f*) in the case of an organization which is regional in scope, the arrangements for ensuring cooperation through the appropriate regional office of FAO, which have been found acceptable after prior consultation with the FAO Member Nations of the region of the other organization, should be incorporated in the agreement.

COOPERATION WITH INTERNATIONAL NON-GOVERNMENTAL ORGANIZATIONS/O

Preamble

1. The ninth session of the Conference[1] noted that experience had shown that with the rapid growth in the number of organizations having relations with FAO it had become necessary to apply strictly the criteria for granting consultative status and specialized consultative status set forth in the FAO Policy concerning Relations with International Organizations (Conference Resolution 37/53).

2. The Conference appreciated, however, that much fruitful cooperation had developed and would continue to develop, particularly at the technical level, between FAO and a considerable number of non-governmental organizations which did not necessitate either consultative or specialized consultative status, and that the support and cooperation of such organizations should be recognized by granting them some form of formal status that would be in keeping with the extent of their association with FAO and its work. Liaison arrangements as a category was inadequate and inappropriate for many organizations whose cooperation was essentially practical and technical.

3. The Conference therefore approved the proposal of the Council that liaison arrangements should be replaced by a new status, designated "liaison status", and that the greater flexibility in its criteria and scope would facilitate the task of appropriately classifying the organizations that have relations with FAO.

---

[1] See paragraph 491 and following paragraphs of the *Report of the ninth session of the Conference.*

RESOLUTION No. 39/57

Establishment of liaison status for international non-governmental organizations

THE CONFERENCE

Takes the view *that liaison arrangements as a category are inadequate and inappropriate for many organizations whose cooperation is essentially practical and technical;* and

Decides that *liaison arrangements shall be replaced by a new status, designated "liaison status", as set forth in Appendix B to this Report.*[1]

[1] The substance of this appendix has been incorporated into the policy statement which follows on pages 175 to 182.

FAO POLICY CONCERNING RELATIONS WITH INTERNATIONAL NON-GOVERNMENTAL ORGANIZATIONS/P

Preamble

1. In implementation of the provisions of the resolution on relationship with non-governmental organizations of the fifth session of the Conference, as amended by Resolution No. 74/51 of the sixth session of the Conference, Resolution No. 37/53 of the seventh session and Resolution No. 39/57 of the ninth session, the arrangements for consultation, cooperation and liaison with international non-governmental organizations shall be established and conducted in the following manner.

Purposes

2. Such arrangements for consultation, cooperation and liaison are intended to enable FAO to secure expert information and advice and technical cooperation and assistance from international non-governmental organizations and to enable organizations which represent important sections of public opinion and are authorities in their fields of professional and technical competence to express the views of their members.

3. Arrangements made with such organizations shall be designed to advance the purposes of FAO by securing maximum cooperation from international non-governmental organizations in the execution of its programme.

Forms of relationship

4. Formal relations with an international non-governmental organization may take one of three forms according to the importance of its field of activity in relation to the activities of FAO, whatever the degree of cooperation envisaged in the common field of activity. These are consultative status, specialized consultative status or liaison status.

General arrangements

5. The Organization established relationships with certain international

non-governmental organizations in order to secure their advice and to associate them effectively with the work of the Organization.

Organizations eligible for consultative status

6. In order to be eligible for consultative status, an international non-governmental organization shall:

(*a*) be international in its structure and scope of activity, be sufficiently representative of the field of interest in which it operates, and be of a recognized standing that renders its views on policy a matter of great interest to governments and to FAO;

(*b*) be concerned with matters covering a substantial portion of FAO's field of activity;

(*c*) have aims and purposes in conformity with the general principles embodied in the Constitution of FAO;

(*d*) have a permanent directing body, authorized representatives and systematic procedures and machinery for communicating with its membership in various countries.

Organizations eligible for specialized consultative status

7. In order to be eligible for specialized consultative status, an international non-governmental organization shall:

(*a*) be international in its structure and scope of activity, and representative of the specialized field of interest in which it operates;

(*b*) be concerned with matters covering a particular portion of FAO's field of activity;

(*c*) have aims and purposes in conformity with the general principles embodied in the Constitution of FAO;

(*d*) have a permanent directing body, authorized representatives and systematic procedures and machinery for communicating with its membership in various countries.

Organizations eligible for liaison status

8. In order to be eligible for liaison status an international non-governmental organization shall:

(*a*) be international in its structure and scope of activity and be sufficiently representative of the field of interest in which it operates;

(*b*) be concerned with matters covering a portion of FAO's field of activity and be in a position to give practical assistance in that field;

(*c*) have aims and purposes in conformity with the general principles embodied in the Constitution of FAO;

(*d*) have a permanent directing body, authorized representatives and systematic procedures and machinery for communicating with its membership in various countries.

Procedure for selecting the organizations with which FAO may enter into formal relationship

9. Before any form of formal relationship is established with an international non-governmental organization, such organization must supply FAO with the information requested by the Director-General.

Consultative status

10. The Conference will at each session examine and take a decision upon the proposals submitted by the Council concerning the organizations seeking consultative status. Consultative status becomes effective upon approval by the Conference and upon acceptance by the organization of the conditions laid down under paragraphs 18, 19 and 20 hereunder. In a year in which there is no Conference session the Council may examine and take a decision on applications for consultative status, subject to review by the Conference at its next session.

11. In deciding upon applications of international non-governmental organizations for consultative status, the Conference will be guided by the following principles:

(*a*) An organization whose primary objectives are related to those of another specialized agency of the United Nations may only be admitted to consultative status after consultation with such agency;

(*b*) Consultative status will not normally be granted to individual organizations that are members of a larger organization authorized to represent them; and, when such an organization is formed, its member organizations shall cease individually to enjoy consultative status.

Specialized consultative status

12. The Director-General may grant specialized consultative status to international non-governmental organizations at his discretion and upon acceptance of the conditions laid down under paragraphs 21 and 22 hereunder. He will report thereon to the Council and consult with the Council when he considers it necessary.

13. In granting applications for specialized consultative status, the Director-General will be guided, as appropriate, by the principles that apply to applications for consultative status (paragraph 11 above).

14. When several international non-governmental organizations are active in any field of FAO's activity, in principle only one should be granted specialized consultative status; no action should be taken until the division or divisions concerned have ascertained which organization is likely to be of most assistance in promoting FAO's objectives. Every opportunity will be taken to encourage such organizations to form themselves into a federation or an association.

Liaison status

15. The Director-General may grant liaison status to international non-governmental organizations at his discretion in accordance with the provisions of paragraph 8 above. He shall report thereon to the Council and will consult with the Council when he considers it necessary.

16. In granting liaison status to international non-governmental organizations, the Director-General will be guided as appropriate by the principles that apply to the granting of consultative status.

Scope of arrangements for consultation, cooperation and liaison

17. An invitation to an FAO meeting and representation thereat by an observer shall not imply the granting to an international non-governmental organization of a status different from that which it already enjoys.

Organizations granted consultative status

18. The privileges of such international non-governmental organizations when

participating in Conference, Council and other meetings shall be those specified in paragraph 3 of Rule XVII of the General Rules of the Organization.

19. An organization in consultative status:

(*a*) shall be entitled to send an observer (without the right to vote) to a session of the Conference and Council, who may be accompanied by advisers; to receive from the Director-General, in advance of the session, all documents bearing on policy or technical questions; to circulate to the Conference its views in writing, without abridgement; to speak before the technical committees of the Conference but not to participate in discussions unless requested by the Chairman; and, upon request addressed to the Director-General and with the consent of the General Committee of the Conference, to speak before the Conference itself;

(*b*) may be invited by the Director-General to participate in experts' meetings, technical conferences or seminars on subjects which fall within its fields of interest, and if it does not so participate it may submit its views in writing to any such meeting or technical conference;

(*c*) will receive non-confidential documentation and information about meetings planned on subjects agreed upon with the Secretariat;

(*d*) may submit, under the authority of its governing body, written statements on programme matters, not exceeding 2 000 words, in one of the languages of FAO, to the Director-General, who may communicate them to the Council.

20. On the other hand, an organization in consultative status shall undertake:

(*a*) to cooperate fully with FAO for the furtherance of the objectives of the Organization;

(*b*) in cooperation with the competent services of FAO, to determine the ways and means of coordinating activities within the field of FAO, with a view to avoiding duplication and overlapping;

(*c*) for this purpose, to invite a representative of the Director-General to attend and participate in the meetings of its governing bodies, general assemblies and appropriate technical meetings, and to arrange for coordination at secretariat level;

(*d*) to contribute, as far as possible, and at the request of the Director-General, to the promotion of a better knowledge and understanding of FAO's programmes and activities through appropriate discussions or other forms of publicity;

(e) to send FAO its reports and publications on an exchange basis;

(*f*) to keep FAO informed of changes in its structure and membership, as well as of important changes in its secretariat.

Organizations granted specialized consultative status

21. An organization in specialized consultative status:

(*a*) shall be entitled to send an observer to appropriate technical meetings with the approval of the Director-General, to receive appropriate publications, and to submit memoranda to the Organization on technical aspects of the FAO programme of mutual specialized interest; it shall be provisionally invited, subject to approval, as appropriate, by the Conference and Council, to send an observer to Conference sessions and in appropriate cases to Council sessions;

(*b*) may be invited by the Director-General to participate in experts meetings, technical conferences or seminars on subjects which fall within its field of interest; and if it does not so participate it may submit its views in writing to any such meeting or technical conference;

(*c*) will receive non-confidential documentation and information about such meetings;

(*d*) may submit to the Director-General, under the authority of its governing body, written statements on programme matters coming within its specialized competence, not exceeding 2 000 words, in one of the languages of FAO, which statements the Director-General may place before the Council.

22. On the other hand, an organization in specialized consultative status shall undertake:

(*a*) to cooperate fully with FAO for the furtherance of the objectives of the Organization within its specialized field;

(*b*) in cooperation with the competent services of FAO, to determine the ways and means of coordinating activities in such specialized field, with a view to avoiding duplication and overlapping;

(*c*) for this purpose, to invite a representative of the Director-General to attend and participate in the meetings of its governing bodies, general assemblies and appropriate technical meetings, and to arrange for coordination at secretariat level;

(*d*) to contribute, as far as possible, and at the request of the Director-General, to the promotion of a better knowledge and understanding of

FAO's programmes and activities through appropriate forms of publicity;

(*e*) to send FAO its reports and publications on an exchange basis;

(*f*) to keep FAO regularly informed of its programme of work, the meetings it plans to hold and of any changes in its structure, membership and secretariat.

Organizations with liaison status

23. The methods and scope of collaboration between an organization that has been granted liaison status and FAO shall be determined and agreed by an exchange of correspondence between such organization and the Director-General.

24. The Director-General may invite organizations in liaison status to send observers to specialized meetings held under the auspices of FAO when he is satisfied that such participation may make a significant contribution to the meeting concerned. The rights of any such observers shall be determined in the aforementioned exchange of correspondence but in no case shall they exceed those accorded to observers of organizations in specialized consultative status.

25. Organizations in liaison status may be invited to send observers to Conference and Council sessions if, in the judgement of the Director-General, there are concrete reasons for inviting them that would forward the technical work of the Organization.

Review of relationship

26. The Conference may terminate arrangements for consultative status which are no longer considered necessary or appropriate in the light of changing programmes or other circumstances. In special cases which may arise between Conference sessions the Council is empowered to terminate such arrangements, subject to review by the Conference.

27. The Director-General may terminate arrangements for specialized consultative status which are no longer considered necessary or appropriate in the light of changing programmes or other circumstances, and will report such action to the Council.

28. An organization in consultative or specialized consultative status which has not shown any interest or has not attended any meetings during a period of two years may be deemed not to have sufficient interest to warrant the continuance of such relationship.

29. The Director-General may terminate arrangements for liaison status which are no longer considered necessary or appropriate by him in the light of changing programmes or other circumstances and shall report such action to the Council.

30. The Director-General shall include in his report to the Conference information on the relations between FAO and international non-governmental organizations established in accordance with the present principles and procedures.

31. The Conference shall review at each session the list of organizations approved for consultative status.

32. The Conference shall review these principles and procedures every two years and shall consider, as necessary, any amendments which may seem desirable.

Granting of observer status[1]

1. At its eighth session the Conference requested the Council to consider and suggest amendments to the Constitution and General Rules of the Organization for the purpose of eliminating any possible ambiguity with respect to the question of observer status, with special reference to the definition of such status, the establishment of criteria for the granting of the status and the consideration of all juridical and practical aspects of the problem.

RESOLUTION No. 44/57

Observer status in respect of international organizations

THE CONFERENCE

Decides:

(*a*) *that in future intergovernmental organizations that do not have an agreement with FAO and non-governmental organizations in liaison status with FAO may be invited to send observers to Conference and Council sessions if, in the judgement of the Director-General, there are concrete reasons for inviting them which would forward the work of the Organization,*

(*b*) *that the status of observers sent to FAO meetings by intergovernmental organizations that have relations with FAO shall not be less than that accorded to the observers of non-governmental organizations in consultative status with the Organization;* and

Notes *that subject to the foregoing interpretation the provisions of the Constitution and General Rules of the Organization which apply to interna-*

Q

[1] Paragraph 497 and Resolution No. 44/57 of the *Report of the ninth session of the Conference*. See also paragraph 2 on page 159 regarding observer status in respect of nations.

tional organizations and the FAO policy statement concerning relations with international non-governmental organizations adopted at its seventh session[1] *provide adequate criteria for the granting of observer status to international organizations and adequately define the status of their observers.*

---

[1] Incorporated in this volume under heading "FAO Policy Concerning Relations with International Non-governmental Organizations": see pages 175 to 182.

PRINCIPLES AND PROCEDURES WHICH SHOULD GOVERN CONVENTIONS AND AGREEMENTS CONCLUDED UNDER ARTICLES XIV AND XV OF THE CONSTITUTION, AND COMMISSIONS AND COMMITTEES ESTABLISHED UNDER ARTICLE VI OF THE CONSTITUTION/R

Preamble

1. The ninth session of the Conference,[1] after considering the report of the Council (C 57/38) came to the conclusion that it was necessary to lay down principles to be adhered to in future whenever the provisions of Articles VI, XIV or XV of the Constitution were being applied. The intention was not to lay down too rigid rules since obviously the text of the various conventions and rules of procedure must be drafted in the light of the desired objectives. The Conference, however, wished to establish a framework, i.e., juridical and administrative norms to govern in future the drafting of new texts or of amendments to existing agreements and of the constituent rules of commissions and committees.

Basic considerations

2. In accordance with the provisions of Article VI of the Constitution, the Conference and the Council may establish general or regional commissions as well as committees and working parties, and may convene general, technical, regional or other meetings. For the necessary juridical act to be accomplished, all that is required is a decision of the Conference or Council.

3. Article XIV of the Constitution applies to conventions and multilateral agreements concluded under the aegis of the Organization. These are agreements concluded between States with respect to which, in conformity with the principles of public international law, the expressed consent of sovereign entities constitutes the required juridical act.

4. However, the procedure of multilateral agreements has been used on several occasions to establish commissions and committees entrusted with specific tasks which fall within the general terms of reference of the Organization.

---

[1] See paragraphs 503 to 509 of the *Report of the ninth session of the Conference*.

5. It must be borne in mind that the express purpose of multilateral agreements is to create contractual obligations for those who become parties to them. Contracting parties undertake to do or not to do certain things, such obligations being generally assumed for a given period. It follows directly from this principle that any agreement concluded under Article XIV of the Constitution among Member Nations of the Organization should entail financial or other obligations going beyond those already assumed under the Constitution of the Organization. Failing this, there would be no grounds for such an agreement, at least not in the legal form prescribed under Article XIV of the Constitution.

6. Hence, any multilateral agreement between Member Governments may undoubtedly provide for the establishment of a commission or an executive body, but this should not be an end in itself since under Article VI the Conference and the Council are empowered to establish such bodies merely by a decision on their part. Consequently, the setting up of a commission or a committee by a multilateral agreement is justified only when such agreement presupposes the assumption of specific obligations going beyond mere participation in the work of the body thus established.

7. It ensues that two sets of principles are required: on the one hand, those governing the preparation, conclusion, entry into force and implementation of a convention or agreement coming within the framework of Article XIV of the Constitution, in other words certain aspects of the law of treaties; and on the other hand, those governing the establishment and the constituent rules of commissions, committees or working parties set up by conventions or agreements or under Article VI of the Constitution (composition, terms of reference, rules of procedure, reporting, etc.).

RESOLUTION No. 46/57

Conventions and agreements, constituent rules of commissions and committees

THE CONFERENCE

1. Considering *that the purpose of conventions and agreements provided for in Article XIV of the Constitution of the Organization is to create new contractual obligations for Member Nations that are parties thereto;*

Declares *that such conventions and agreements should be concluded only when they entail for the contracting parties obligations going beyond those assumed under the Constitution of the Organization.*

2. Considering *further the desirability of avoiding in future inconsistencies and inadequacies in the texts of conventions and agreements concluded under Article XIV of the Constitution of the Organization and of securing greater uniformity in the provisions of such conventions and agreements and in the procedure for the preparation of texts and their submission to the Conference or Council of the Organization for approval;*

Resolves *that the principles embodied in Appendix D to this Report*[1] *shall in future govern the drafting of conventions and agreements and be taken into account by the Conference and Council when approving such conventions and agreements.*[2]

3. Considering *the desirability of ensuring consistency and uniformity with respect to the constituent rules of commissions, committees, subcommissions, subcommittees established under Article VI or Article XIV of the Constitution;*

Noting *that the activities of these bodies must be in conformity with the policy of the Organization;*

Resolves *that the principles embodied in Appendix D to this Report shall govern the constituent rules of existing commissions, committees, subcommissions and subcommittees established under Article VI of the Constitution and those to be established in future under that Article and that these principles shall govern the drafting of the constituent rules of bodies to be established in future under Article XIV of the Constitution.*[3]

4. Recognizing *the necessity of amending the Constitution and General Rules of the Organization in the light of the present Resolution;*

Adopts *the amendments given in Appendix I to this Report;*[4] and

Urges *the parties to existing conventions and agreements and the members of the bodies established thereunder to apply as far as possible the rules contained in the present statement of principles and reflected in the amendments to the Constitution and General Rules of the Organization appearing in*

---

[1] Appendix D to the *Report of the ninth session of the Conference* appears in this volume on pages 189 to 199.

[2] The delegate for the Netherlands reserved the position of his Government with respect to the binding force of this Resolution. The delegates for the United Kingdom and Yugoslavia wished to record their understanding that this Resolution was to be interpreted in the light of the statement contained in paragraph 1 above.

[3] See footnote 2 to paragraph 2 of this Resolution.

[4] For Appendix I, see the *Report of the ninth session of the Conference*, pages 260 to 321.

Appendix I to this Report; and

Invites *these parties to amend the texts of these conventions and agreements when feasible in order to bring them into line with said principles and amendments.*

Semi-independent bodies

8. The Conference noted that the provisions of the statutes of certain bodies were a cause of confusion regarding their legal status. There was some doubt as to whether these bodies should be considered as entirely independent entities with only working relations with the Organization or as bodies having been established within the framework of the Organization under Articles VI, XIV or XV of the Constitution. The lack of clarity regarding the relationship of these entities with the Organization and, consequently, the extent and character of the responsibility of the Organization with respect to these bodies were a cause of concern to the Conference.

RESOLUTION No. 47/57

Semi-independent bodies

THE CONFERENCE

Considering *the desirability of avoiding any ambiguity regarding the legal status of bodies promoted by the Organization;*

Resolves *that in future bodies utilizing the Secretariat services of the Organization shall be set up either:*

(*a*) *under Article VI or Article XIV of the Constitution and the relevant Rules; or*

(*b*) *under Article XV of the Constitution in which case the relationship of such bodies to the Organization shall in each instance be clearly defined; or*

(*c*) *entirely outside the framework of the Organization and as such completely independent, any cooperation or coordination to be developed through a relationship agreement to be approved by the Council and Conference under Rule XXIV.4 (c) of the General Rules of the Organization and Article XIII of the Constitution, which agreement shall make any servicing by the Organization subject to the programme, financial procedures and operations of such bodies being consistent with and in furtherance of the objectives of the Organization.*

Appendix[1]

PRINCIPLES AND PROCEDURES WHICH SHOULD GOVERN CONVENTIONS AND AGREEMENTS CONCLUDED UNDER ARTICLES XIV AND XV OF THE CONSTITUTION, AND COMMISSIONS AND COMMITTEES ESTABLISHED UNDER ARTICLE VI OF THE CONSTITUTION

A. Principles to govern conventions and agreements

Terminology

1. Such treaties concluded under Article XIV of the Constitution as are of a worldwide scope shall in future be designated by the term "convention", while the others shall be designated by the term "agreement".

2. The word "constitution" shall in future be reserved to designate the Constitution of the Organization and the term "statutes" shall be utilized only to designate the collection of constituent rules of bodies established under Article VI of the Constitution, which expression shall include the terms of reference, reporting procedures, rules of procedure, etc.

3. In future, the term "council" shall be used only to designate the Council of the Organization. Bodies established by conventions or agreements under Article XIV of the Constitution shall be called "commissions" or "committees", and their subsidiary bodies "subcommissions", "subcommittees" or "working parties".

Participation in conventions and agreements

4. Method of participation: Both the traditional system, i.e., that of signature, signature subject to ratification, and accession, as well as the more recent and simplified system of acceptance by the deposit of an instrument of acceptance have in the past been applied by the Organization and shall be retained. Under both systems the period during which nations may become parties to the conventions or agreements may be limited by a provision in the basic text if circumstances so warrant.

---

[1] Appendix D of the *Report of the ninth session of the Conference* as amended by Resolution No. 8/91 of the twenty-sixth session of the Conference.

Preamble

5. The preamble shall always specify that the convention or agreement is established within the framework of the Organization. It shall in addition clearly state the purposes and objectives of the convention or agreement, which purposes and objectives must be in line with those of the Organization.

6. The preamble should not contain information regarding the drafting parties or the dates of approval of the instrument by the drafting meeting or by the Council or Conference. The date of approval by the competent authority of the Organization should be given in the body of the instrument or in the testimonium.

Participation of Associate Members

7. Existing bodies established under conventions and agreements shall be invited to amend their basic instrument, if and when necessary, in order to make participation by Associate Members possible.

Amendments

8. Conventions and agreements shall contain, when appropriate, provisions reflecting the following principles:

(*a*) Amendments to all conventions and agreements concluded under Article XIV of the Constitution shall be reported to the Council which shall have the power to disallow them if it finds that such amendments are inconsistent with the objectives and purposes of the Organization or the provisions of the Constitution. If the Council considers it desirable, it may refer these amendments to the Conference which shall have the same power. In addition, such amendments shall be subject to prior approval by at least a two-thirds majority of all the parties to the convention or agreement. Amendments to conventions and agreements which do not provide for the establishment of a body shall be submitted to an advisory committee prior to consideration by the Council.

(*b*) Amendments are operative until disallowed by the Council or the Conference.

(*c*) Amendments involving new obligations for the contracting parties shall come into force in respect of each contracting party only on acceptance by it. The instruments of acceptance of amendments involving new obligations shall be deposited with the Director-General of the Organization who shall inform all the contracting parties of the receipt of acceptances and the entry into force of amendments.

(*d*) Conventions and agreements shall contain a provision regarding the position of contracting parties that do not accept amendments.

Entry into force of conventions and agreements

9. Uniformity regarding the number of participations required in order to bring a convention or agreement into effect is not necessary. All texts shall indicate the method of determining the effective date of participation. Notification of participation shall be dispatched by the Director-General to all signatory, acceding and accepting parties and to all Member Nations of the Organization in accordance with Rule XXI.3 of the General Rules of the Organization, as well as to the Secretary-General of the United Nations in conformity with the Regulations to give effect to Article 102 of the Charter of the United Nations.

Reservations

10. A clause on the admissibility of reservations may be inserted in conventions and agreements. Any such clause shall be in line with public international law as reflected in particular in the provisions of Part II, Section 2 of the Vienna Convention on the Law of Treaties of 1969. Failing such a clause, the admissibility of reservations shall be governed by public international law as reflected in the above provisions of the Vienna Convention. The Director-General of the Organization shall notify all signatory, acceding and accepting governments of all reservations.

Territorial application

11. Each convention and agreement shall contain a clause regarding its territorial application in order to avoid any ambiguity in this respect. The contracting parties shall, at the time of signature, ratification, accession or acceptance, declare explicitly to what territories the convention or agreement shall extend, especially in those cases where a government is responsible for the international relations of more than one territory. In the absence of such a declaration, the convention or agreement shall be deemed to apply to all the territories for the international relations of which the nation is responsible. Subject to the principles laid down in paragraph 14 and to any relevant provision of the convention or agreement regarding withdrawal, the scope of the territorial application may be modified by a subsequent declaration.

Supplementary agreements

12. Nations that are not parties to a basic convention or agreement may become parties to a supplementary agreement. However, if participation in the basic convention or agreement is restricted to Member Nations of the Organization, non-member States which are members of the United Nations, any of its specialized agencies or the International Atomic Energy Agency may become parties to the supplementary agreement only if the basic instrument provides for such a possibility.

Interpretation and settlement of disputes

13. Each convention and agreement shall contain a suitable provision regarding its interpretation and settlement of disputes. Among alternative procedures for settlement of disputes are conciliation, arbitration, or reference to the International Court of Justice. The nature of the provision for settlement of disputes should be determined in the individual convention or agreement by the character and objective of the particular instrument involved.

Withdrawal and denunciation

14. (*a*) All conventions and agreements drafted in future shall contain a clause regarding withdrawal or denunciation on the basis of the following principles:

(*i*) No participating nation may withdraw before having been a party to the convention or agreement for a certain period. Uniformity is not necessary with respect to the duration of this period or the required advance notice.[1]

(*ii*) A nation that is responsible for the international relations of more than one territory shall, when giving notice of its withdrawal from a convention or agreement, state to which territory or territories the withdrawal is to apply. In the absence of such a declaration the withdrawal shall be deemed to apply to all the territories for the international relations of which the nation concerned is responsible, with the exception of Associate Members.

(*iii*) A nation may give notice of withdrawal with respect to one or more of the territories for the international relations of which it is responsible.

[1] The representative of Japan reserved his position with respect to this provision.

(*b*) Some of the existing conventions and agreements provide for participation either of:

(*i*) Member Nations only, or

(*ii*) Member Nations and non-member nations, the participation of the latter being subject to approval of the body established under such convention or agreement and of the Conference or Council of the Organization.

Any Member Nation that gives notice of withdrawal from the Organization is deemed to have simultaneously given notice of withdrawal from such conventions or agreements and this withdrawal is deemed to apply to all the territories for the international relations of which the Member Nation is responsible. A clause dealing with this aspect of the participation shall be incorporated in all conventions and agreements of this nature drafted in future, having regard to the principles contained in paragraph 3 (*b*) of Article XIV of the Constitution.

Termination

15. All conventions and agreements shall contain a termination clause. This clause shall *inter alia* provide for automatic termination if and when the number of participants drops below that required to bring it into force, unless the remaining participants unanimously decide otherwise. The system of termination by a qualified majority decision of the participants shall be discontinued. It is understood that, after a convention or agreement has been in force for a given number of years, the participants thereto should, upon recommendation of the Conference or Council of the Organization as appropriate, consider the desirability either of maintaining the convention or agreement or of terminating it by withdrawal.

Authentic languages

16. Unless otherwise decided by the Conference or Council, all conventions and agreements shall be drawn up in English, French and Spanish, which languages shall be equally authentic.

Depositary functions

17. Greater uniformity shall be introduced into the text regarding the notifications which the Director-General is required to make as the depositary of conventions and agreements. These notifications shall be made to all

signatory, acceding or accepting governments. In addition, one certified copy of the text of each convention or agreement shall be transmitted to each Member Nation of the Organization and to such non-member nations as may become parties to the convention or agreement, in accordance with Article XIV.7 of the Constitution, and all Member Nations of the Organization shall be informed of each participation in accordance with Rule XXI.3 of the General Rules of the Organization.

B. Principles to govern the constituent rules of commissions and committees[1]

Establishment of subsidiary bodies

18. Under Rule XXXII.1[2] of the General Rules of the Organization, commissions, committees and working parties set up in pursuance of Article VI of the Constitution may establish subcommissions, subcommittees and subsidiary working parties.

19. The texts of all conventions or agreements establishing commissions or committees under Article XIV of the Constitution shall specify whether such commissions or committees may establish subsidiary bodies.

20. Both with respect to Article VI and Article XIV bodies, the convention or agreement, or statutes as the case may be, shall make the establishment of subsidiary bodies subject to the availability of necessary funds in the relevant approved budget. When the related expenses are to be borne by the Organization, the determination of such availability shall be made by the Director-General. Before taking any decision involving expenditure in connection with the establishment of subsidiary bodies, the body concerned must have before it a report from the Director-General on the administrative and financial implications thereof.

Purpose and functions

21. Article VI.3 of the Constitution as amended in 1955 states that the Conference or Council when establishing commissions, committees and working parties must determine their "terms of reference".

---

[1] See Addendum I to this Appendix, page 201.
[2] Now Rule XXXV.1.

22. As regards bodies established prior to 1955, the Conference noted that the purpose of these bodies and their functions or terms of reference were in some instances omitted from the relevant resolution or were vague. These resolutions should therefore be reviewed by the Conference or Council.

Eligibility for membership and observer status

23. Membership in the commissions and committees provided for in Article VI of the Constitution shall not be open to non-member nations of the Organization.

24. Membership in a regional commission established under Article VI of the Constitution is open to all Member Nations and Associate Members whose territories are situated wholly or partly in the region. However, in order to be considered as a member of the commission the eligible Member Nation or Associate Member shall communicate to the Director-General a formal expression of intention.

25. As regards Member Nations and Associate Members whose metropolitan territories are not situated in a given region, a broad interpretation shall be given to the provisions of Article VI in that any Member Nation that is responsible for the international relations of any non self-governing territory in the region considered shall be eligible for membership in the commission of that region and that any Member Nation or Associate Member that has a special interest in the work of a commission for that region may, upon its request, participate in the work of that commission in the capacity of observer.

26. The statutes of commissions and committees established under Article VI of the Constitution and the conventions and agreements setting up commissions or committees under Article XIV of the Constitution shall contain provisions regulating the question of observer status for non-member nations of the Organization in accordance with the statement of principles relating to the granting of observer status to nations (see Appendix C to this Report[1]).

27. Conventions and agreements establishing commissions and committees under Article XIV of the Constitution shall provide that Member Nations and Associate Members of the Organization that are not members of such commissions and committees may, upon their request, be represented by an observer at sessions of these commissions and committees.

---

[1] Appendix C to the *Report of the ninth session of the Conference* appears in this volume on pages 161 to 164.

Relations with international organizations

28. The relations between commissions or committees established under Article VI and other international organizations shall be governed by Article XIII of the Constitution and Rule XXIV.4 (*c*) of the General Rules of the Organization, as well as by the rules adopted by the Conference on the matter of relationship with international organizations. These provisions shall likewise govern the relations between commissions and committees established by conventions and agreements under Article XIV of the Constitution and other international organizations.

Relations with governments

29. Commissions and committees established under Article VI and Article XIV of the Constitution should, in principle, not be empowered to enter into arrangements with governments which are not members of the commission or committee. When this, however, is found desirable, a specific provision shall be incorporated in the statutes, convention or agreement, as the case may be, indicating the scope of such authority and specifying that all such arrangements shall be made by the Director-General of the Organization.

Reporting and recommendations

30. Provision shall be made in the relevant texts to the effect that commissions, committees and other bodies established under Article VI or Article XIV of the Constitution, as well as their subsidiary bodies, shall transmit their reports and recommendations to the Director-General, those of the subsidiary bodies to be transmitted through the parent body. In the case of bodies referred to in paragraph 33 (*c*), provision may also be made in the relevant texts to the effect that recommendations or decisions not having financial, policy or programme implications for the Organization, may be transmitted directly to the members of the body concerned for their consideration and action.

The Director-General shall:

(*a*) take these reports into account when preparing the Programme of Work and Budget of the Organization;

(*b*) bring to the attention of the Conference through the Council any recommendations adopted by these bodies which have policy implications or which affect the programme or finances of the Organization;

(*c*) include in his annual statement to the Conference an analysis of the work done by these bodies.

31. It is understood that, pending such formal action, the Director-General will circulate these reports to all members of the bodies concerned and to all Member Nations and Associate Members of the Organization for their information. The policy, programme and financial implications for the Organization of these reports shall be acted upon by the appropriate governing body of the Organization.

Administrative and financial matters

32. The statutes of bodies established under Article VI of the Constitution and the basic texts of bodies established under Article XIV of the Constitution shall specify that:

(*i*) the financial operations of such bodies shall be governed by the appropriate provisions of the Financial Regulations of the Organization, subject to the terms of paragraph 33 (*iii*) below;

(*ii*) the expenses of members of such bodies or of experts attending sessions of these bodies as government representatives are to be borne by the respective governments and the expenses of experts attending in their individual capacity are to be borne either by the budget, if any, of the body concerned, or by the Organization;

(*iii*) the Secretary of each body shall be appointed by the Director-General and shall be administratively responsible to him. In the case of bodies referred to in paragraph 33 (*c*), the basic texts may specify that the Secretary shall be appointed by the Director-General after consultation with, or with the approval or concurrence of, the members of the body concerned.

(iv) non-member nations of the Organization that become members of bodies established by conventions or agreements concluded under Article XIV of the Constitution shall be required to contribute towards the expenses incurred by the Organization with respect to the activities of these bodies.

33. Bodies established under Article XIV of the Constitution fall into one of the three following categories:

(*a*) bodies entirely financed by the Organization;

(*b*) bodies that, in addition to being financed by the Organization, may undertake cooperative projects financed by members of the body;

(*c*) bodies that, in addition to being financed by the Organization, have autonomous budgets.

Bearing in mind the obligations of the Organization, the following principles shall be observed and appropriate provisions shall be inserted in the text of conventions and agreements:

(*i*) contributions for cooperative projects and autonomous budgets shall be remitted to the Organization. The Organization shall establish in each case a trust or special fund into which these contributions shall be paid and these funds shall be administered by the Organization in accordance with the Financial Regulations and Rules of the Organization;

(*ii*) any financial regulations adopted by such bodies shall be consistent with the principles embodied in the Financial Regulations of the Organization and be reported to the Finance Committee which shall have the power to disallow such financial regulations or amendment if it finds that they are inconsistent with the principles embodied in the Financial Regulations of the Organization;

(*iii*) expenses borne by the Organization shall be determined and paid within the limits of the relevant item of the budget of the Organization as approved by the Conference.

Amendments to basic resolutions

34. Bodies established under Article VI may suggest amendments to the basic resolution by which they were set up and which determined their terms of reference. Any proposals for such amendments must be transmitted to the Director-General in time for inclusion in the agenda of the Council or Conference as appropriate.

Rules of procedure

35. Conventions and agreements establishing commissions and committees under Article XIV of the Constitution shall provide that the rules of procedure and amendments thereto adopted by such commissions and committees shall not be inconsistent with the convention or agreement establishing the body or with the Constitution. For the adoption of rules of procedure or amendments

thereto, the required majority within the commissions and committees shall be uniformly set at two thirds of the membership of the body.

36. Rules of procedure of subcommissions, subcommittees or subsidiary working parties of bodies established under Articles VI and XIV shall be approved by these bodies and shall be in conformity with the rules of procedure of these bodies and the General Rules of the Organization.

Sessions

37. The site and date of all sessions of bodies and their subsidiary bodies established under Articles VI and XIV of the Constitution shall be determined in consultation with the Director-General, and the relevant texts shall contain a provision regarding this requirement.[1]

Quorum, majority and voting arrangements

38. The required quorum and majority for taking decisions shall be provided for in the basic instruments concluded under Article XIV and the statutes of bodies established under Article VI of the Constitution. The quorum, voting arrangements and proceedings at meetings shall be governed by the provisions of Rule XII of the General Rules of the Organization.

Executive committee

39. The establishment of an executive committee, when provided for, shall be stated in the basic instruments or in the statutes of the bodies concerned. As regards the composition of executive committees, the Conference noted that in the case of Article XIV bodies they sometimes comprise as many as three Vice-Chairmen and in one instance the outgoing Chairman. In cases where the expenses of such officers, when performing duties related to the work of the body, are to be borne by the Organization, the number of Vice-Chairmen should be limited.

Agenda

40. The rules of procedure of all bodies under Article VI shall specify that the agendas of their meetings shall be drawn up by the Director-General in consultation with the Chairman.

---

[1] See Addendum II to this Appendix, page 204.

Semi-independent bodies

41. The Conference, having noted that the statutes of the International Poplar Commission and the International Chestnut Commission were ambiguous regarding their legal status, recommended that the Director-General approach these commissions in order to clarify the situation. The Director-General should report to the Council on the outcome of these consultations and recommend whether they should be classified as bodies established under Articles VI, XIV or XV of the Constitution of the Organization, or considered as entirely independent entities in accordance with Resolution 47/57. In the latter case, draft agreements between the Organization and these commissions regarding their relationship with the Organization and their servicing by the Organization should be submitted to the Council on the understanding that such agreements would be in conformity with the provisions of the Constitution and Rules of the Organization as interpreted in this document, and should set out clearly the responsibility of the Director-General, in order that the Council, when considering the agreements, may be made fully aware of their implications.

Agreements between the Organization and Member Governments

42. The Conference considered the case of independent entities that have been or are being established by agreements between the Organization and a government, such as the Regional Forestry School as well as the Regional Forestry Research Centre, both for the Near East, and decided that no subsidiary body of the Organization should participate in the capacity of board of directors in the administration of an institution over which the Conference does not have full control. Under certain circumstances, however, it might be desirable for the Director-General to be a member of the board of directors of such an institution.

43. Specific draft agreements for the establishment of independent entities should be referred to the Committee on Constitutional and Legal Matters for consideration prior to submission to the Council and Conference of the Organization.

Addendum I

EXCERPT FROM THE REPORT OF THE THIRTEENTH SESSION OF THE FAO CONFERENCE (1965): PARAGRAPHS 418 TO 429 ON COMMITTEES, WORKING PARTIES AND PANELS OF EXPERTS

418. In 1961 the Conference requested the Council to undertake a study of FAO's expert committees and panels, pointing out that "while this was a useful method of working, care should be taken to ensure that such groups or panels should only be set up for specific purposes and only for the length of time required to accomplish their main purpose, so that they may not develop into permanent bodies".

419. In accordance with the recommendations of the Programme Committee which had studied the matter on behalf of the Council, the Council submitted its recommendations to the Conference (C 65/32).

420. The Conference *welcomed* the Council's report, which it considered would assist considerably in achieving greater coordination, and *confirmed* these recommendations, namely:

(*a*) adherence to the nomenclature used in Article VI of the Constitution;

(*b*) amendment of Rule XXXI as set out below;[1]

(*c*) effective and economical application of the system of panels and expert committees;

(*d*) application of the internal machinery proposed by the Director-General.

421. With regard to the nomenclature to be used, the Conference *reiterated its earlier request* that only the nomenclature used in Article VI of the Constitution be used in regard to bodies set up by FAO. In particular, the Conference *agreed* that for bodies set up under paragraphs 2 and 4 of Article VI, the following should apply:

(*a*) "*Committee*" applies to committees of selected Member Nations or As sociate Members set up to study and report on matters pertaining to the purpose of the Organization;

---

[1] Now Rule XXXV. The amended text has been incorporated in the *Basic Texts* of the Organization.

(*b*) "*Working Party*" applies to working parties of selected Member Nations or Associate Members set up to study and report on matters pertaining to the purpose of the Organization;

(*c*) "*Panel of Experts*" is a list of experts selected in their individual capacity on the basis of their expert knowledge, to give advice on specific subjects by correspondence and/or by participation in meetings of some or all of them;

(*d*) "*Committee of Experts*" and

(*e*) "*Working Party of Experts*": these terms apply to groups of experts selected in their personal capacity. Whether or not their members are drawn from a panel of experts, they can only be established on the authority of the Conference or the Council. They are governed by Rule XXXI.3[1] of the General Rules of the Organization, which limits the duration of the term of office of their members.

422. While recognizing that special problems arise when bodies are set up or sessions convened jointly with other United Nations agencies or intergovernmental organizations, the Conference urged that every effort should be made to avoid confusion and adhere as far possible, even in such cases, to the nomenclature established by FAO.

423. Attention was also drawn to departures from the established nomenclature in the case of bodies established under certain programmes, such as *Codex Alimentarius*, and requested the Director-General to ensure that bodies established under such programmes adhere to FAO practices.

424. With regard to the establishment of panels of experts or committees and working parties of experts, attention was drawn to the terms of Article VI.4 of the Constitution, whereby the Director-General consults with Member Nations, Associate Members and National FAO Committees on the establishment of panels of experts. Similarly, attention was drawn to Article XIII.4 and Rule XXXIV[2] of the General Rules regarding the procedure to be followed to secure proper consultation with governments in regard to relations between the Organization and national institutions or private persons.

425. With regard to conferences or sessions to which both governments and individuals or national institutions were invited, the Conference *requested* the

[1] Now Rule XXXV.4.
[2] Now Rule XXXVIII.

Director-General to ensure that the requirements of the above provisions were also applied.

426. The Conference noted that the Council had emphasized the need for continuing and careful scrutiny of the complex of bodies and panels of experts appointed in their personal capacity on the one hand, and of ad hoc committees and working parties of government representatives on the other, to ensure the best use of the Organization's resources. The Conference *requested* the Council to undertake a review of all such bodies and panels of experts over a four-year cycle, to ensure that these bodies are maintained only for the length of time required to accomplish their main purpose and do not develop into permanent bodies.

427. The Conference also *requested* the Director-General to avoid proliferation of such committees, working parties or panels of experts and to avoid duplication of functions with existing bodies, either within the Organization or established by other agencies.

428. The Conference *welcomed* the Director-General's initiative regarding the internal supervisory machinery established by him to ensure the implementation of the foregoing proposals, as set out in document C 65/32, paragraph 17 (*a*), (*b*), (*c*), (*d*).

429. The Conference agreed that for convenient reference the foregoing paragraphs dealing with committees, working parties and panels of experts should be incorporated in the next edition of the *Basic Texts*, Volume II.

Addendum II

RESOLUTION No. 21/67 OF THE FOURTEENTH SESSION OF THE CONFERENCE

Sessions of FAO commissions, committees and working parties and of their subsidiary bodies

THE CONFERENCE

Noting *the recommendation of the United Nations ad hoc Committee to Examine the Finances of the United Nations and Specialized Agencies, to the effect that no dependent body should be permitted to increase the number of length of its sessions already authorized without the specific approval of the organ which established it;*

Considering *that this recommendations as regards its implementation with respect to FAO, should be construed as applying to commissions, committees and working parties of Member Nations and of experts established under Articles VI and XIV of the FAO Constitution, and their subsidiary bodies, as well as to subsidiary bodies of committees of the Council established under Article V;*

Recognizing *that a literal implementation of the aforementioned recommendation of the ad hoc Committee would result in serious practical difficulties;*

Realizing *however that the objectives of such recommendation can be achieved by the exercise of appropriate controls by the Conference and Council;*

Aware *that the procedures under which FAO operates require advance approval by the Conference of the Programme of Work and Budget for the subsequent biennium, and that the Programme of Work and Budget for 1968-69 includes a complete list of sessions of statutory bodies and subsidiary bodies and of other conferences and consultations which the Director-General proposes for the biennium (C 67/3-Sup 1-Rev. 1);*[1]

---

[1] The Conference noted that certain minor modifications had been agreed to during the debates and requested that these approved changes be included in this document, which would be revised and circulated to governments as soon as possible after the Conference had concluded the adoption of its report on the Programme of Work for 1968-69.

Decides *that sessions of FAO bodies, other than those sessions listed in the Programme of Work for the relevant biennium, should only be convened in exceptional circumstances;*

Authorizes *the Director-General to make such exceptions when in his view such action is necessary for the fulfilment of the Programme of Work as approved by the Conference, subject however to such exceptions being reported to the session of the Council immediately following such action;*

Invites *Member Governments to draw the attention of their delegates attending sessions of bodies of Member Nations to the need to adhere to the schedule of sessions provided for in the approved Programme of Work;*

Decides *that the terms of this Resolution shall apply equally to the convening of unscheduled sessions of panels of experts established under Article VI.4 of the Constitution;*

Decides *that in the case of new bodies to be established under Article VI of XIV of the Constitution, or subsidiary bodies established by the latter, a provision should be included in the convention, agreement, statutes or rules of procedure, as appropriate, limiting the frequency and duration of sessions of such bodies; and that the statutes of existing bodies should be amended accordingly as opportunity arises;*

Further decides *that the Committee on Commodity Problems and the Committee on Fisheries should include similar limitations in the statutes of any new subsidiary bodies which they may establish; and that the statutes of existing subsidiary bodies be amended accordingly as opportunity arises;*

Requests *the Director-General to bring this Resolution to the attention of the chairmen and members of bodies of experts and, if necessary, also of intergovernmental bodies, in the event of any proposals formulated by them to convene unscheduled sessions.*

(Adopted 21 November 1967)

Addendum III

RESOLUTION No. 12/79 OF THE TWENTIETH SESSION OF THE CONFERENCE

Procedures for the establishment and abolition of statutory bodies

THE CONFERENCE

Noting *that at its Seventy-fourth Session the Council recommended that the Conference adopt a resolution to the effect than any proposal to establish a new body under Articles VI, XIV or XV of the Constitution should be accompanied by a document prepared by the Director-General, setting forth certain details for consideration by the Conference or Council as appropriate, before authorizing the establishment of any new body under those Articles of the Constitution;*

Noting further *that the Council requested the Committee on Constitutional and Legal Matters (CCLM) to examine the wording of a proposed operative paragraph of such resolution, and also to consider the question whether provisions could be made in the Organization's* Basic Texts *for the abolition of bodies established under Articles VI, XIV or XV, which were either inactive or had outlived their usefulness;*

Considering *that the Council had examined these matters at its Seventy-fifth Session in the light of the CCLM's report thereon;*

Concurring *with the recommendations of the Seventy-fifth Session of the Council;*

1. Decides *that the following procedures shall be followed in connection with the establishment of new bodies under Articles VI, XIV or XV:*

(i) *Any proposal to establish a new body under Articles VI, XIV or XV of the Constitution shall be accompanied by a document prepared by the Director-General setting forth in detail:*

 (a) *the objectives that are to be achieved through the establishment of the body;*

 (b) *the manner in which the body will carry out its functions and any impact that its creation may have on the current or future programmes;*

(c) *the financial implications of the establishment of the body for the current biennium, as well as a forecast of the financial implications for the future biennia.*

(ii) (a) *Before approving or authorizing the establishment of any new body under Article VI of the Constitution, the Conference or as appropriate the Council shall consider the document referred to in paragraph (i) above.*

(b) *Where the Director-General establishes a body under the authority provided for in paragraph 6 of Article VI of the Constitution, he shall submit to the Council the document described in paragraph (i) above, together with his report on the action taken in accordance with paragraph 6 of Article VI.*

(iii) (a) *Before a technical meeting or conference comprising Member Nations participates in the drawing up of a draft convention or agreement for submission to the Council or Conference as foreseen in paragraph 3 (a) of Article XIV of the Constitution, such technical meeting or conference shall consider the document referred to in paragraph (i) above.*

(b) *Where, after consideration of such document, the technical meeting or conference suggests to the Conference or Council that the convention or agreement be approved and submitted to Member Nations concerned for acceptance, the Conference or Council shall consider the document referred to in paragraph (i) above, appropriately revised as necessary, before approving the convention or agreement.*

(iv) (a) *Before the Conference takes any policy decision as to whether the Director-General should be authorized to negotiate an agreement as foreseen under paragraph 2 of Article XV the Conference shall consider the document referred to in paragraph (i) above.*

(b) *Where, after consideration of such document, the Conference authorizes the Director-General to negotiate an agreement, the Conference or Council before approving such agreement in accordance with paragraph 3 of Article XV shall consider the document referred to in paragraph (i), appropriately revised as necessary.*

2. Requests *the Regional Conference to review carefully the functioning of the regional bodies in their respective regions with a view to determining whether they are functioning effectively in the service of Member Nations, and to recommend any necessary measures in that connection.*

3. Requests *the Director-General to keep the activities of bodies established under Articles VI, XIV or XV under review in the light of their reports, and, if he is of the opinion that such a body is either inactive or has outlived its usefulness, to recommend that the Council or Conference:*

(i) exercise its authority to abolish bodies established under Article VI or subsidiary bodies thereof,

(ii) invite States, parties to conventions or agreements concluded under Article XIV or XV, to consider terminating such convention or agreement by withdrawal in accordance with the relevant provisions thereof,

(iii) exercise its authority to effect the withdrawal of the Organization from bodies established under Article XV.

4. Requests *the Director-General to include the present resolution in Section R of Volume II of the* Basic Texts *of the Organization.*

(Adopted 27 November 1979)

Resolution No. 14/69 of the fifteenth session of the Conference[1]

AUTHORITY, TERMS OF REFERENCE AND CONSTITUTIONAL STATUS OF REGIONAL CONFERENCES/S

FAO regional conferences

THE CONFERENCE

Noting *the growing importance of the role of regional conferences in the elaboration of the general policy of the Organization;*

Considering *the desirability, in line with Article VI.5 of the Constitution, of laying down the terms of reference of the regional conferences, so that they may more effectively carry out their role;*

Considering further *the recommendation of the Ninth Regional Conference for the Near East (Baghdad, September-October 1968) and the resolution of the Fifth Regional Conference for Africa (Kampala, November 1968);*

Decides *that regional conferences for Africa, Asia and the Far East,*[2] *Europe, Latin America*[3] *and the Near East shall have the following functions:*

(a) *to hold consultations at a high level;*

(b) *to indicate the special problems of their respective regions and the priority areas of need which should be taken into account in preparing the Programme of Work and Budget for the next biennium as well as in relation to longer-term programme objectives;*

(c) *to examine the adaptation of the policy objectives of the Organization to the needs of the region concerned;*

(d) *to undertake consultations on the means by which the countries in the*

---

[1] The above resolution has been incorporated in this volume in accordance with the decision of the fifteenth session of the Conference (see paragraph 600 of the *Report of the fifteenth session of the Conference*, Rome 1969).

[2] Title changed by decision of the twentieth session of the Conference to "Regional Conference for Asia and the Pacific" (see paragraph 461 of the *Report of the twentieth session of the Conference*, Rome 1979).

[3] Title changed by decision of the twenty-second session of the Conference to "Regional Conference for Latin America and the Caribbean" (see paragraph 326 of the *Report of the twenty-second session of the Conference*, Rome 1983).

region can help solve their own problems through the use of their own resources, and on the volume and nature of the external aid required to implement their food and agricultural development plans;

Decides further *that regional conferences may make recommendations to Member Nations in the region, the Conference, the Council, the Director-General and, through the Director-General, to the United Nations regional economic commissions. Recommendations addressed to the Conference, the Council and the Director-General will be studied by the Director-General, who will inform the Council and the Conference as to how far he has been able to take them into account in framing his draft Programme of Work and Budget and, where he has been unable to do so, state his reasons; and*

Recommends:

(a) *that the regional conferences for Africa, Asia and the Far East,*[1] *Europe, Latin America*[2] *and the Near East be held at intervals of not less than two years, in the years in which the Conference does not meet in regular session;*

(b) *that, with a view to strengthening collaboration among regional development agencies, the agenda for the regional conferences and for the United Nations regional economic commissions should in each case be the subject of consultations between FAO and these commissions.*

(Adopted 24 November 1969)

---

[1] Title changed by decision of the twentieth session of the Conference to "Regional Conference for Asia and the Pacific" (see paragraph 461 of the *Report of the twentieth session of the Conference*, Rome 1979).

[2] Title changed by decision of the twenty-second session of the Conference to "Regional Conference for Latin America and the Caribbean" (see paragraph 326 of the *Report of the twenty-second session of the Conference*, Rome 1983).

FAO POLICY REGARDING ASSISTANCE IN ESTABLISHING REGIONAL RESEARCH AND TRAINING INSTITUTES/T

Preamble

1. The ninth session of the Conference[1] had before it a note from the Director-General requesting policy guidance regarding FAO assistance in the establishment of regional research and training institutes and containing a proposed course of action. The Conference noted that several regional bodies of FAO had recommended the establishment of such institutes to meet needs for research and training in specific subject fields common to several countries of a region. The Conference noted also that several countries had recently offered sites and various facilities and had requested the Organization to assist in the establishment and operation of research and training institutes on a regional basis.

2. Since a number of aspects of the Director-General's proposal required clarification and further consideration, the Conference adopted the following resolution:

RESOLUTION No. 48/57

Regional research and training institutes

THE CONFERENCE

Having noted *the considerable number of proposals for FAO assistance in the establishment of regional research and training institutes;*

Recognizing *the desirability of providing the Director-General with more specific policy guidance in dealing with this matter than is contained in the Constitution;*

Desiring *clarification upon certain aspects of the matter and opportunity for further study of the Director-General's proposal;*

---

[1] See paragraphs 511 and 512 of the *Report of the ninth session of the Conference*.

Requests *the Council to consider this proposal in its meeting immediately following the ninth session of the Conference and advise the Director-General on a suitable course of action.*

Council action[1]

3. At the ninth session of the Conference, the Director-General requested policy guidance regarding FAO assistance in the establishment of regional research and training institutes. The Conference noted that several regional bodies of FAO had recommended the establishment of such institutes, while several member countries had offered sites and facilities and had requested the Organization to assist in the establishment and operation of research and training institutes on a regional basis. The Conference had requested the Council to consider the matter and to advise the Director-General on a suitable course of action (Resolution No. 48/57). The Council, at its twenty-eighth session, in turn requested the Committee on Constitutional and Legal Matters to examine the constitutional and legal aspects, and the Programme Committee to examine the policy issues, with a view to considering the technical aspects at its twenty-ninth session (Resolution No. 1/28).

4. The twenty-ninth session of the Council had before it the report of the first session of the Committee on Constitutional and Legal Matters and the reports of the first and second sessions of the Programme Committee. Both committees accepted that three general classes of research and training institutes existed, viz.:

(*a*) institutes managed and financed solely by individual Member Governments primarily to serve their own nationals;

(*b*) institutes so managed and financed, but which would welcome additional financial support in return for their recognition as regional institutes for the training of nationals of countries in the region;

(*c*) new institutes specifically established as regional institutes.

The Council agreed that institutes of the first type were outside the scope of the study requested by the Conference, although many of them undertook the training of fellows under the fellowship schemes sponsored by FAO. As regards the second and third types, the Council considered that, subject to the provisos noted in paragraphs 6 to 10 following, FAO support for, and participation in, such regional research and training institutes should be permitted on the following conditions:

[1] See paragraphs 71 to 78 of the *Report of the twenty-ninth session of the Council.*

(*i*) The Director-General must be satisfied that the purpose of the proposed institute is in accordance with the aims and objectives of the Organization and that the technical standards of research to be applied will make a continuing contribution to the development of knowledge in the field in which the institute is to operate. In the case of training institutes, he will satisfy himself that there is a generally felt need in participating countries for the training envisaged, and that instruction will be of a standard that will ensure a real contribution to the supply of trained personnel. Emphasis should be placed upon applied research to find solutions to practical problems faced in a number of countries. Training should be in line with the current and prospective need for trained personnel.

(*ii*) The government of the country in which the institute is located must guarantee to provide the land, buildings and equipment locally available, although it might enter into special arrangements with other interested governments for financing this requirement. In addition, the host country would share in providing staff and funds to meet maintenance and operating costs. Further, the host government must undertake to request within its technical assistance country target, and over a number of years, those goods and services which FAO agrees to provide as described in paragraph 5 below.

(*iii*) The host country must agree to the operation of the institute under a governing body composed of representatives of all contributing countries, with FAO serving in an advisory capacity.

(*iv*) A sufficient sum of money should be pledged by interested governments (including the host government), to be paid annually over a period of years, to assure the continuing operation of the institute on a sound financial basis.

5. The Council also agreed that, subject to the foregoing requirements, FAO participation might involve:

(*a*) advising on the organization and programme of work of the institute, not only at its inception but on a continuing basis as required;

(*b*) undertaking to include in its Technical Assistance Programme, or endeavouring to obtain from the Special Projects Fund, a contribution in goods and services to an amount agreed upon between the host country and FAO each year at the time the ETAP[1] country programme is negotiated, as a contribution towards the cost of operations of the institute during that year, unless there should be an increase in the Technical Assistance Funds that can be used for regional projects to a level that would allow inclusion, within the FAO regional projects total, of the cost of goods and services for a regional institute or institutes, thus making it unnecessary to include this sum within any particular country target.

6. The Council considered the principles which should govern the conditions of support and, where required, the forms of agreement which would be appropriate between the Organization and (*a*) governments of member countries which were participating in the establishment and/or maintenance of such regional institutes; and (*b*) the governing bodies of such regional institutes.

7. The Council noted that, where funds from the Organization's regular budget were involved, short-term assistance might be arranged by the Director-General, subject to budgetary approval by the Conference, although the view was expressed that any such allocation from the regular budget should only be made exceptionally.

8. The Council recognized that certain forms of support were already provided for under the conditions laid down by intergovernmental agencies furnishing technical assistance as, for example, under the Expanded Technical Assistance Programme and under the United Nations Special Fund for Economic Development.[1] The Council agreed that in such circumstances it would be appropriate for the necessary arrangements to be made between the Director-General and the government or governments concerned. Such arrangements would be in pursuance of the provisions of Article I.3 (*a*) of the FAO Constitution. In regard to the Expanded Technical Assistance Programme, they would be in line with the relevant resolution passed by the Conference, and in regard to the United Nations Special Fund for Economic Development, they would be in line with the intentions of the fund as noted in the relevant resolution of the United Nations General Assembly (Resolution No. 1240 [XIII], paragraphs 39 to 44).

9. In regard to assistance to regional research and training institutes, furnished through FAO by private foundations, or from any other voluntary contributions, the Council noted that these would fall within the provisions of Financial Regulation 6.7.

---

[1] Now United Nations Development Programme.

10. Subject to paragraphs 6 and 7 above, the Council agreed that, whenever long-term financial commitments were involved, either on the part of the Organization itself, or through the Organization, of individual Member Nations, arrangements for assistance should be subject to the control of the Conference and Council as provided for in either Article XV or XIV of the Constitution respectively. In such circumstances the Council recommended that the principles set out in Appendix III of the Report of the first session of the Committee on Constitutional and Legal Matters, as reproduced in Appendix B to this report,[1] be used by the Director-General as guidance in drafting the necessary agreements for submission to the Conference.

[1] Appendix B to the *Report of the twenty-ninth session of the Council* appears in this volume on pages 216 to 222.

Appendix[1]

GUIDING PRINCIPLES WITH RESPECT TO AGREEMENTS UNDER ARTICLE XV OF THE CONSTITUTION FOR THE ESTABLISHMENT OF INTERNATIONAL INSTITUTIONS DEALING WITH QUESTIONS RELATING TO FOOD AND AGRICULTURE

Preamble

Agreements for the establishment of regional institutions should include the following points, it being understood that the pattern given below would have to be modified, adapted or completed to suit specific situations.

Basic considerations

1. *Aims and objectives*

The statutes should spell out the purposes and objectives of the institution and these should be in conformity with those of the Organization. The relationship with FAO should also be clearly defined.

2. *Organs*

The organs of the institutions should comprise a governmg body and a director. All governments parties to the basic instrument should be members of the governing body. The functions of the governing body should not be entrusted to an FAO organ. The Director-General of FAO should be represented on the governing body in a purely advisory capacity. The functions of the governing body should include the approval of an annual programme of work and budget as submitted by the director of the institution.

3. *Administration*

The administration of each institution should be placed under the authority of the director appointed by the governing body after consultation with the Director-General of FAO. The director should have full authority to administer the activities of the institution and should be its legal representative in all transactions. The conditions of appointment of the director should be determined by the governing body.

---

[1] Appendix B to the *Report of the twenty-ninth session of the Council.*

4. *Staff*

The staff of the institution should be recruited by and responsible to the director. The responsibility of the staff should be international in character.

5. *Obligations of parties*

(*a*) Host government: provision of land, buildings, premises, maintenance, protection, public utilities, etc.

(*b*) Governments parties to the agreement including host government: financing in accordance with arrangements made at the time of the negotiation of the agreement.[1]

(*c*) FAO: contributions in terms of technical staff or consultants, goods, fellowships and other possible services; conceivably also grants-in-aid.

The agreement should specify the number of years over which the assistance of FAO would be forthcoming.

6. *Control by FAO*

The control of FAO could be exercised, *inter alia*, by one or more of the following methods:

(*a*) Representation of the Director-General in an advisory capacity on the governing body of the institution.

(*b*) Obligation on the part of the institution to submit periodically to the Organization a technical, administrative and financial report on the work of the institution.

(*c*) Submission of the programme of work and budget of the institution to the Organization for comments or approval.

(*d*) Management of the funds and/or control of all the financial operations of the institution by FAO.

(*e*) Approval by FAO of by-laws (e.g., financial regulations, rules of procedure and staff regulations).

(*f*) The relations between institutions and international organizations to be governed by the relevant provisions of the FAO Constitution and the

[1] In the case of a bilateral agreement between FAO and the host government, these provisions would have to be modified accordingly or deleted.

General Rules of the Organization as well as by the rules adopted by the Conference on the matter of relationships with international organizations, all such relations to be dealt with by the Director-General.

(*g*) The institutions should in principle not be empowered to enter into arrangements with governments which are not members of the Organization. When this, however, is found desirable, a specific provision should be incorporated in the agreement indicating the scope of such authority and specifying whether such arrangements should be made by the Director-General of the Organization.

(*h*) The question of observer status for non-member governments of the Organization should be governed by the statement of principles relating to the granting of observer status to nations, adopted by the ninth session of the Conference.

A policy decision would have to be taken in every individual case as to the nature and scope of the control.

7. *Expenses*

The expenses of members of the institution or of experts attending meetings of the institution as government representatives should be borne by the respective governments, and the expenses of experts attending in their individual capacity should be borne by the budget of the institution.

8. *Legal status*

The agreement should contain a clause to the effect that the institute is to be recognized as an international foundation and is to have the capacity of a legal person to perform any legal act appropriate to its purpose which is not beyond the powers granted it by the agreement. It should also contain a clause stipulating that FAO does not assume any civil, financial, or other responsibility other than those provided for in the agreement. The agreement should also contain a clause regarding the privileges and immunities to be enjoyed by the institute, the members of the governing body and the staff.

9. *Method of participation in agreement*

Participation in the agreement may be effected either through the traditional system, i.e., that of signature, signature subject to ratification, and accession, or by the more recent and simplified system of acceptance by the deposit of an instrument of acceptance. Under both systems, the period during which nations may become parties to the agreement could be limited, if circumstances so warranted.

10. *Amendments to agreement*

(*a*) Amendments should require Council approval unless the Council considers it desirable to refer the amendments to the Conference for approval. In addition, such amendments should be subject to prior approval by at least a two-thirds majority of the parties to the agreement.

(*b*) Amendments should not become operative before approval by the Council or the Conference. The actual date on which they come into force should be specified in the text.

(*c*) Amendments involving new obligations for the contracting parties should come into force in respect of each contracting party only on acceptance by it. The instruments of acceptance of amendments involving new obligations should be deposited with the Director-General of the Organization, who should inform all the contracting parties of the receipt of acceptances and the entry into force of amendments.

(*d*) Agreements should contain a provision regarding the position of contracting parties who do not accept the amendments.

11. *Entry into force*

The agreement should indicate the number of participations required in order to bring it into force, as well as the method for determining the effective date of participation. Notification of participation should be dispatched by the Director-General to all signatory, acceding and accepting parties, and to all Member Nations of the Organization.

12. *Reservations*[1]

A reservation clause should be inserted in the agreement, and this clause should state that a reservation may become operative only upon unanimous acceptance by the parties to the agreement. Failing such acceptance, the nation concerned should not become a party to the agreement. With respect to reservations made prior to the coming into force of the agreement, such reservations would have to be accepted by all the nations which at the time of the coming into force of the agreement were parties thereof. For calculating the

[1] In the case of a bilateral agreement between FAO and the host government, these provisions would have to be modified accordingly or deleted.

number of acceptances of the agreement necessary to bring it into force, nations having made reservations should not be included in this number. Reservations made after the coming into force of the agreement would have to be accepted by all parties to the agreement. The Director-General of the Organization should notify all signatory, acceding and accepting governments of all reservations. Governments not having replied within three months from the date of notification should be considered as having accepted tacitly the reservation, and the notification referred to above should draw attention to this rule.

13. *Territorial application*

The agreement should contain a clause regarding its territorial application. The contracting parties should at the time of signature, ratification, accession or acceptance declare explicitly to what territories the agreement shall extend, especially in those cases where a government is responsible for the international relations of more than one territory. Subject to the provisions laid down in paragraph 15, and to any relevant provision of the agreement regarding withdrawal, the scope of the territorial application may be modified by a subsequent declaration.

14. *Interpretation and settlement of disputes*

Each agreement should contain a suitable provision regarding its interpretation and the settlement of disputes.

15. *Withdrawal and denunciation*

The agreement should contain a clause regarding withdrawal or denunciation on the basis of the following principles:

(*a*) No participating nation may withdraw before having been a party to the agreement for a certain period.

(*b*) A nation that is responsible for the international relations of more than one territory shall, when giving notice of its withdrawal, state to which territory or territories the withdrawal is to apply.

(*c*) A nation may give notice of withdrawal with respect to one or more of the territories for the international relations of which it is responsible. Each agreement shall contain a clause dealing with the position of Member Nations as regards their participation in the agreement as the result of their withdrawal from membership in the Organization.

16. *Termination*[1]

The duration of each agreement should be specified in the agreement. The agreement should contain a termination clause, which clause should, *inter alia*, provide for automatic termination if and when the number of participants drops below that required to bring it into force, unless the remaining participants unanimously decide otherwise.

17. *Authentic languages*

Unless otherwise decided by the Conference, the agreements should be drawn up in English, French and Spanish, which languages would be equally authentic.

18. *Procedures governing preparatory work and approval by the Conference*

In addition to the provisions of Article XV of the Constitution and Rule XXXI.3 (*c*)[2] of the General Rules of the Organization, the following provisions of Article XIV of the Constitution and Rule XXI of the General Rules of the Organization should apply, *mutatis mutandis*, to the agreement concluded under Article XV of the Constitution:

Article XIV of the Constitution[3]

Par. 3 (*b*). Inclusion in the agreement of a provision regarding the Member Nations and non-member nations that can become parties to the agreements;

Par. 3 (*c*). Safeguard regarding financial obligations for Member Nations that are not parties to the agreement;

Par. 4. Entry into force of the agreement;

Par. 5. Participation by Associate Members;

Par. 7. Authentic text and registration with the United Nations.

---

[1] In the case of a bilateral agreement between FAO and the host government, these provisions would have to be modified accordingly or deleted.

[2] Now Rule XXXIV.3 (*c*).

[3] The paragraphs below summarize the original text.

Rule XXI of the General Rules of the Organization[1]

Par. 1 (*a*). Notification by the Director-General to Member Nations of proposed agreement, and submission of reports on technical, administrative and financial implications with request for comments;

Par. 1 (*b*). Consultation with the United Nations, other specialized agencies and with other international and regional organizations in related fields, as the case may be;

Par. 1 (*c*). The agreement should specify the nature and degree of relationship with FAO and that reports on the activities of the institute should be transmitted to the Director-General of the Organization for the information of the Conference;

Par. 3. Submission of approved text to governments, with a view to their acceptance;

Par. 4. Full powers to government representatives to sign the agreement;

Par. 5. Report by the Director-General to the FAO Conference on entry into force, etc., of agreement.

[1] The paragraphs below summarize the original text.

ALPHABETICAL INDEX/U

U

ALPHABETICAL INDEX/U

Abbreviations used in index:

Const. VI.2, 6 (10, 10-11)	Constitution: Article VI, paragraphs 2 and 6, pages 10, 10-11
GR. XXIV.3 (*b*) (56)	General Rules of the Organization: Rule XXIV, paragraph 3, subparagraph (*b*), page 56
FR. 12.8 (107)	Financial Regulations 12, paragraph 8, page 107
RC. I.2 (113)	Rules of Procedure of the Council, Rule I, paragraph 2, page 113
PC. II.2 (118)	Rules of Procedure of the Programme Committee, Rule II, paragraph 2, page 118
FC. IV.3 (125)	Rules of Procedure of the Finance Committee, Rule IV, paragraph 3, page 125
CCP. III.3 (*a*) (128)	Rules of Procedure of the Committee on Commodity Problems, Rule III, paragraph 3, subparagraph (*a*), page 128
COFI. III.3 (*c*) (135)	Rules of Procedure of the Committee on Fisheries, Rule III, paragraph 3, subparagraph (*c*), page 135
COFO. VII.3 (143)	Rules of Procedure of the Committee on Forestry, Rule VII, paragraph 3, page 143
COAG. IV.2 (147)	Rules of Procedure of the Committee on Agriculture, Rule IV, paragraph 2, page 147
CFS. III (151)	Rules of Procedure of the Committee on World Food Security, Rule III, page 151
Vol. II (167)	Volume II, page 167

A

B

C

D

E

F

L

N

S

T

U

V

FAO MEMBERSHIP
(180 Members as at November 2000)

Countries	Effective date of membership
Afghanistan	1 December 1949
Albania	12 November 1973
Algeria	19 November 1963
Angola	14 November 1977
Antigua and Barbuda	7 November 1983
Argentina	27 November 1951
Armenia	8 November 1993
Australia	16 October 1945
Austria	27 August 1947
Azerbaijan	20 October 1995
Bahamas	8 November 1975
Bahrain	8 November 1971
Bangladesh	12 November 1973
Barbados	6 November 1967
Belgium	16 October 1945
Belize	7 November 1983
Benin	9 November 1961
Bhutan	7 November 1981
Bolivia	16 October 1945
Bosnia and Herzegovina	8 November 1993
Botswana	1 November 1966
Brazil	16 October 1945
Bulgaria	6 November 1967
Burkina Faso	9 November 1961
Burundi	19 November 1963
Cambodia	11 November 1950
Cameroon	22 March 1960
Canada	16 October 1945
Cape Verde	8 November 1975
Central African Republic	9 November 1961
Chad	9 November 1961
Chile	17 May 1946
China	16 October 1945
Colombia	17 October 1945
Comoros	14 November 1977
Congo	9 November 1961
Cook Islands	11 November 1985
Costa Rica	7 April 1948
Côte d'Ivoire	9 November 1961
Croatia	8 November 1993
Cuba	19 October 1945
Cyprus	14 September 1960
Czech Republic	6 November 1993
Democratic People's Republic of Korea	14 November 1977
Democratic Republic of the Congo	9 November 1961
Denmark	16 October 1945
Djibouti	14 November 1977
Dominica	12 November 1979
Dominican Republic	16 October 1945
Ecuador	16 October 1945
Egypt	16 October 1945
El Salvador	19 August 1947
Equatorial Guinea	7 November 1981
Eritrea	8 November 1993
Estonia	11 November 1991
Ethiopia	1 January 1948
European Community - Member Organization	26 November 1991
Fiji	8 November 1971
Finland	27 August 1947
France	16 October 1945
Gabon	9 November 1961
Gambia	22 November 1965
Georgia	20 October 1995
Germany	27 November 1950
Ghana	9 November 1957
Greece	16 October 1945
Grenada	8 November 1975
Guatemala	16 October 1945
Guinea	5 November 1959
Guinea-Bissau	26 November 1973
Guyana	22 August 1966
Haiti	16 October 1945
Honduras	16 October 1945
Hungary	6 November 1967
Iceland	16 October 1945
India	16 October 1945
Indonesia	28 November 1949
Iran (Islamic Republic of)	1 December 1953
Iraq	16 October 1945
Ireland	3 September 1946
Israel	23 November 1949
Italy	12 September 1946
Jamaica	13 March 1963
Japan	21 November 1951
Jordan	23 January 1951
Kazakhstan	7 November 1997
Kenya	27 January 1964
Kiribati	15 November 1999
Kuwait	9 November 1961
Kyrgyzstan	8 November 1993
Lao People's Democratic Republic	21 November 1951
Latvia	11 November 1991
Lebanon	27 October 1945
Lesotho	7 November 1966
Liberia	16 October 1945
Libyan Arab Jamahiriya	24 November 1953
Lithuania	11 November 1991
Luxembourg	16 October 1945
Madagascar	9 November 1961
Malawi	22 November 1965
Malaysia	9 November 1957
Maldives	8 November 1971
Mali	9 November 1961
Malta	5 October 1964
Marshall Islands	12 November 1999
Mauritania	9 November 1961
Mauritius	12 March 1968
Mexico	16 October 1945
Mongolia	12 November 1973
Morocco	13 September 1956
Mozambique	14 November 1977
Myanmar	11 September 1947

FAO MEMBERSHIP
(180 Members as at November 2000)

Countries	Effective date of membership	Countries	Effective date of membership
Namibia	14 November 1977	Slovakia	6 November 1993
Nepal	27 November 1951	Slovenia	8 November 1993
Netherlands	16 October 1945	Solomon Islands	11 November 1985
New Zealand	16 October 1945	Somalia	17 November 1960
Nicaragua	26 October 1945	South Africa	9 November 1993
Niger	9 November 1961	Spain	5 April 1951
Nigeria	11 October 1960	Sri Lanka	21 May 1948
Niue	12 November 1999	Sudan	13 September 1956
Norway	16 October 1945	Suriname	26 November 1975
Oman	8 November 1971	Swaziland	8 November 1971
Pakistan	7 September 1947	Sweden	13 February 1950
Palau	12 November 1999	Switzerland	11 September 1946
Panama	16 October 1945	Syrian Arab Republic	27 October 1945
Papua New Guinea	8 November 1975	Tajikistan	20 October 1995
Paraguay	30 October 1945	Thailand	27 August 1947
Peru	17 June 1952	The Former Yugoslav Republic of Macedonia	9 November 1993
Philippines	16 October 1945	Togo	23 May 1960
Poland	9 November 1957	Tonga	7 November 1981
Portugal	11 September 1946	Trinidad and Tobago	19 November 1963
Qatar	8 November 1971	Tunisia	25 November 1955
Republic of Korea	25 November 1949	Turkey	6 April 1948
Republic of Moldova	20 October 1995	Turkmenistan	20 October 1995
Romania	9 November 1961	Uganda	19 November 1963
Rwanda	19 November 1963	United Arab Emirates	12 November 1973
Saint Kitts and Nevis	7 November 1983	United Kingdom	16 October 1945
Saint Lucia	26 November 1979	United Republic of Tanzania	8 February 1962
Saint Vincent and the Grenadines	7 November 1981	United States of America	16 October 1945
Samoa	12 November 1979	Uruguay	30 November 1945
San Marino	12 November 1999	Vanuatu	7 November 1983
Sao Tome and Principe	14 November 1977	Venezuela	16 October 1945
Saudi Arabia	23 November 1948	Viet Nam	11 November 1950
Senegal	9 November 1961	Yemen	22 May 1990
Seychelles	14 November 1977	Zambia	22 November 1965
Sierra Leone	9 November 1961	Zimbabwe	7 November 1981